Designlicious

GASTRONOMY BY DESIGN

BASHEER
GRAPHIC BOOKS

Chapters

Foreword

What we eat says the most about us—our culture, habits, philosophy, experiences—but we've rarely taken the time to understand or appreciate the design and effort that goes into preparing, packaging or presenting the food we consume every day.

In recent times, instances of home delivered gourmet food, "concept" food products, eateries with cutomisable menus, and even real time video streaming of your home ordered food being prepared, are increasingly common. It is also increasingly important that the need to stand out amongst competition does not necessarily translate into garish or tacky designs that attract more attention than needed. In light of this, *Designlicious* aims to bring the reader back to basics by showcasing work that successfully focus on a brand's strengths and philosophy, and how it is communicated through clever and simple design solutions.

For the discerning, this book is a spotlight on the importance of designing successful visual identities, from points of purchase, interior design, food packaging, table setting and typography, to countless details that often go unnoticed. These handpicked projects were selected based on how effective their designs were in terms of: communicating the character and essence of the brand, displaying a strong understanding of their target audience, market and product, and having a special visual appeal or "yummy factor".

In the following pages, you will be tempted by gorgeous mood-setting photography and deceptively simple design, accompanied by dashes of information that will make you want to go out there and start experiencing food again.

We hope that the foodie in you will be inspired to step out and allow yourself to be transformed by design, the truly invisible hand that moulds our daily experiences. Neither a book solely about design nor just about food, *Designlicious* is nothing short of a gastronomic triumph. So sit back, relax, and savour.

What's in a Name?

Designing a successful visual identity in the competitive industry of food involves more details than just a simple logo, tagline and complementary colours. From the typography on chopping board menu to monster graphics on cups, this chapter compiles the most deliciously designed visual identities that are dedicated to the love of food.

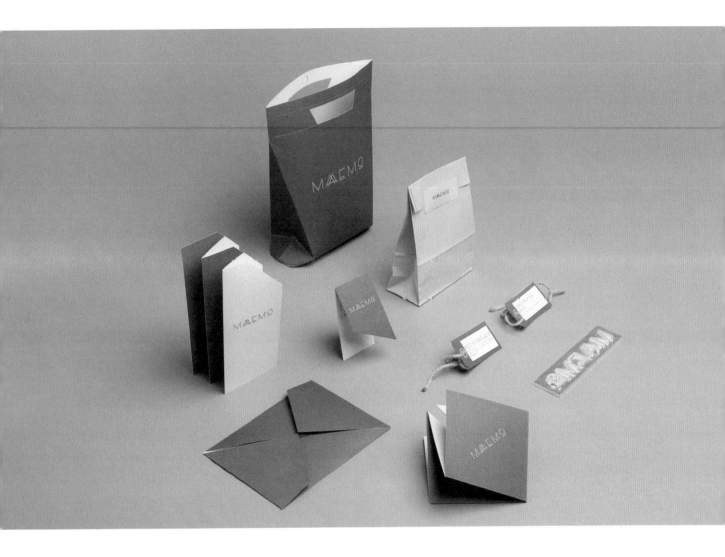

Maaemo

design studio
Uniform Strategic Design

design
Ludvig Bruneau Rossow, Torgeir Hjetland

Maaemo is an ecological gourmet restaurant in Oslo, Norway. The fact that the restaurant has a Norwegian owner, Danish cook and Finnish sommelier, speaks of its truly Scandinavian collaboration. The cuisine of Maaemo is Nordic with its name and colour scheme derived from the Finnish word for "Mother Earth"—soil is nurtured by clear, ice blue water to create life.

The visual identity of Maaemo is inspired by Scandinavian nature and architecture which is apparent in the lines, shapes and lighting thus creating poetic Nordic modernist theme. Such a sense is achieved through the consistency of shape and colour, incorporating features such as a classic Danish designer chair and a pendulum lamp in its interiors. With a philosophy that incorporates both function and aesthetics, Maaemo's menu, folder, letterhead and bill are stripped of decoration, and left with clean and functional lines, complementing the restaurant's interior décor.

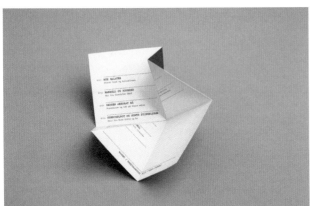

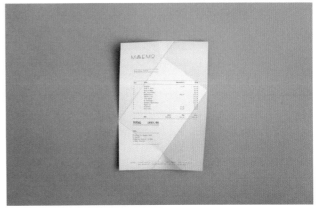

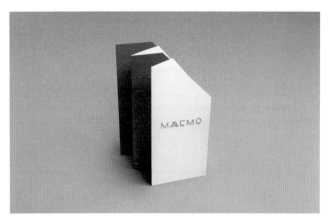
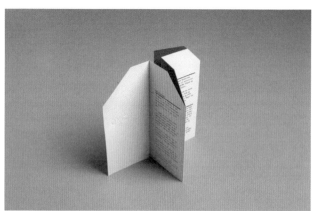
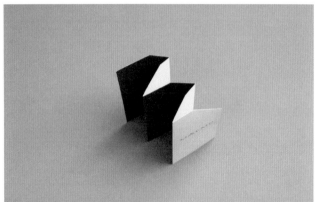
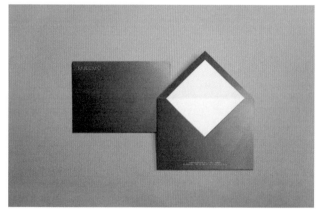

Das Neue Kubitscheck

design studio
Designliga

design
Sasa Stanojčić, Christina Koepf,
Andreas Döhring, Nadine Schüssel

photography
Designliga (Communication Material)
Pascal Gambarte (Interior Design)

Munich's West-end district houses a cross-section of social classes including migrant workers, intelligentsia, students and trade people coexisting in mutual understanding and respect.

"Tell me what music you listen to, and I'll tell you who you are" was among the principles that served as a blueprint, starting-point and road-map for the look and feel of the café's marketing campaign. Subsequently, the name "Das Neue Kubitscheck" (The New Kubitscheck) was implemented deliberately for its political allusions. Multifaceted, dynamic and free from rigid frameworks, this café's design intended to be vibrant and in a state of permanent flux and change. This way, it adopts to developments instead of aligning itself with convenient ideas. An impact is definitely made to whoever picks up the menu or journal which features bold, provocative statements and images.

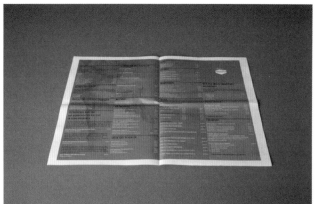

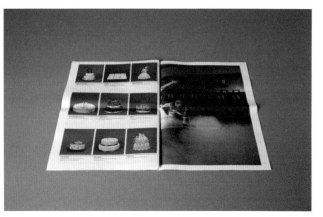

All About Tea

design studio
Moving Brands

photography
Adam Laycock

All About Tea is an expert wholesale tea distributor based in Portsmouth, UK. Their tea is sourced from remote regions with offerings that extend from classic varieties to specialist blends.

To stand out from its competitors, All About Tea's identity needed to appeal to the existing wholesale market, and increasingly to retail channels. Inspired by the brand's passion for tea, expedient delivery services and respect for high quality, the visual identity incorporates various symbols that represent these strengths. The laser-cut dots of the logo represent the process of blending and straining tea while its circular form references iconic industry standard seals.

The type is set in Garamond which lends itself to the quirks and passion of the company.

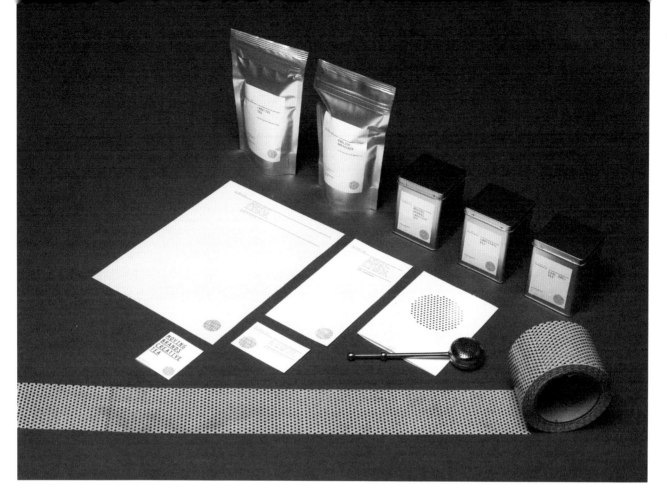

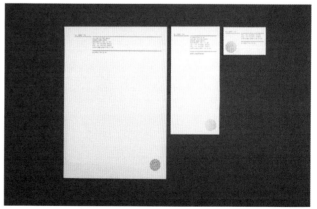

PROPER
TEA
SERVED
HERE

OUR TEA IS SUPPLIED
BY ALL ABOUT TEA

TEA BLENDERS AND
PACKERS OF PORTSMOUTH

*Proper tea has flavour, colour,
richness and strength. That's what
makes it so refreshing.*

*You have just found a proper cup
of tea. We only serve tea from the
master blenders: All About Tea.*

Step inside for total refreshment.
ALLABOUTTEA.CO.UK

ALL ABOUT TEA

Aki Nagao

design studio
Commune

art direction
Ryo Ueda

design
Ryo Ueda, Manami Inoue, Naohiro Iwamoto

photography
Kei Furuse [GAZEfotographica]

interior design
Takashi Kuwabara [mangekyo], Yuiko Kodama [mangekyo]

copywriting
Kousuke Ikehata

web direction
Fumiaki Hamagami [Imaginary Stroke]

printing direction
Manami Sato, Atsuhiro Kondo

Aki Nagao is a French restaurant whose concept is "Every Day's French". Offering high quality French cuisine but avoiding being too prestigious and elitist, it adopts a more casual and welcoming approach. As owner and chef, Aki Nagao, draws from all his experiences and background in his dishes, the design expresses the spirit of the restaurant as his DNA. Using the DNA structure as a recurring motif for the logo, sign and name cards, the visual identity aims to make a strong impression on customers.

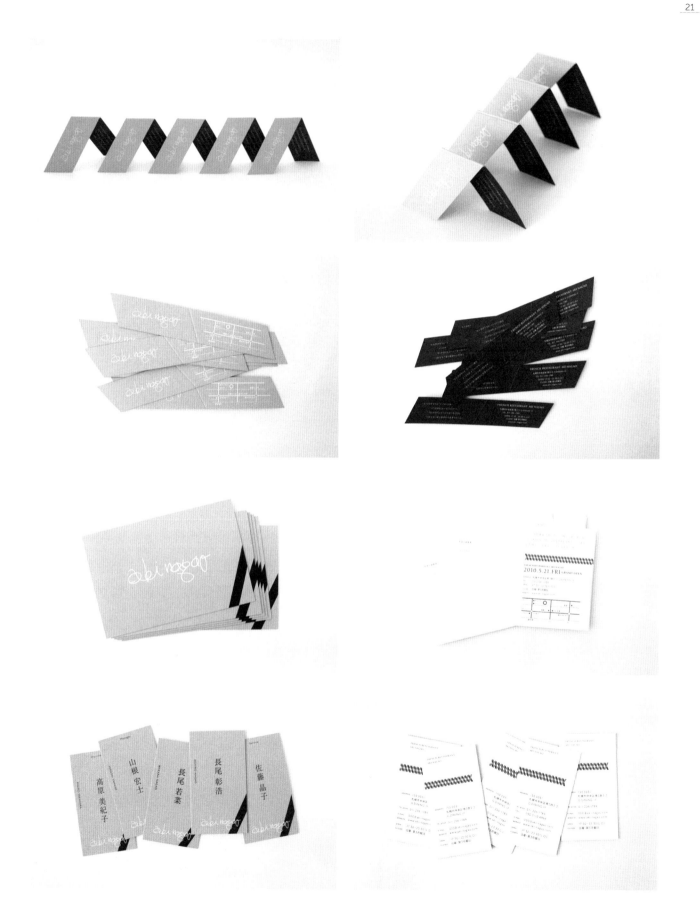

5º Pino

design studio
LoSiento

design
Borja Martinez

photography
LoSiento

The graphic identity for 5º Pino, a café as well as a restaurant, draws from the English translation of its name: 5ᵗʰ Pine. Inspired by this, all finishes of the interiors seek an organic feel in terms of material and appearance. The main use of wood is a significant allusion to the forest, in particular, the pine forest.

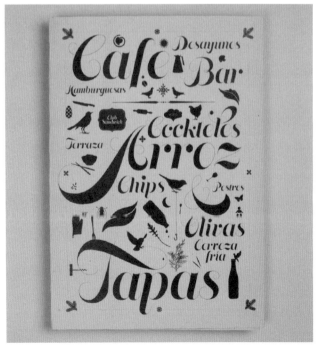

Cocotte

design studio
Foreign Policy Design Group

creative & art direction
Yah-Leng Yu

design
Yah-Leng Yu

photography
Michael Tan (Mika Images)

design & craft production
Tianyu Isaiah Zheng (TY)

web design
Bryan Lim

web developer
Motoshi Goto

Cocotte is a French restaurant located in the fascinating Little India neighbourhood in Singapore. The food is unpretentious home-style cooking in communal sharing portions. The Cocotte logo takes its inspiration from old-style local French eateries and hand-painted signage. Rough-looking weathered menu boards with newsprint menus to further convey the simplicity, the down-to-earth and unpretentious personality.

Crespella

design studio
Tag Collective

design
Becca Eley

photography
Poul Ober

Designed by Tag Collective, Crespella is an Italian crêpe and espresso bar located in Park Slope, Brooklyn. Its identity design aims to convey its classic and sophisticated style with an edgy Italian attitude.

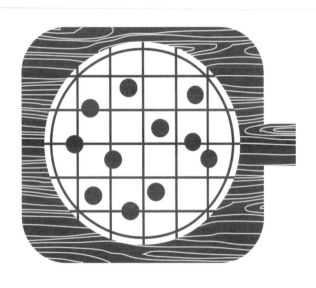

THE SQUARE CUT. GIVING YOU THE ILLUSION OF EATING LESS, WHILE ENJOYING MORE. **BRILLIANTLY YUMMY.**

SURE WE'RE PROUD OF OUR DARTS AND BOWLING TROPHIES, BUT MSP BEST PIZZA! **C'MON, FORGET ABOUT IT!**

Carbone's Pizzeria

design studio
Sussner Design Company

creative direction
Derek Sussner

design
Brandon Van Liere

copywriting
Jeff Mueller is Floating Head

Carbone's Pizzeria is a pizza franchise in Minnesota. Based on research, its primary customers were females aged 39 who grew up ordering pizza from Carbone's. Hence, the tagline "Carbone's Pizzeria, A Slice of the Neighbourhood Since 1954" was coined to imply quality and familiarity. The designers selected a logo from the various ones the pizzeria adopted over the years, and polished it to be adaptable for reproduction in print, embroidery and signage. Next in the refinement of its visual identity was a carefully selected colour palette, art patterns, icons and product photography. With these design elements in place, new interior and exterior signage, menus, screen-printed posters, t-shirts, promotion collateral and a website was created.

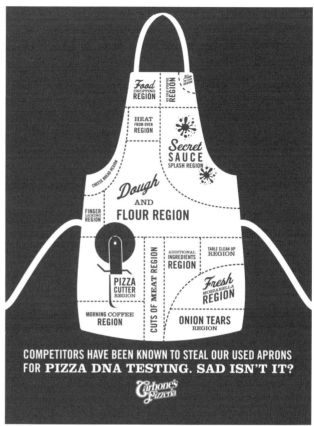

COMPETITORS HAVE BEEN KNOWN TO STEAL OUR USED APRONS FOR **PIZZA DNA TESTING. SAD ISN'T IT?**

YOU KNOW THOSE FOAM *Cheese* HEADS WISCONSINITES WEAR? **HA! OURS ARE ACTUAL CHEESE.**

THE CARBONE'S *Secret* SAUCE SIMMERS SAFELY, SECURELY AND **SCRUMPTIOUSLY IN THE LOCK POT.**

East Bay Café

design studio
Turnstyle

creative direction
Steven Watson

design
Steven Watson

East Bay Café is an on-campus cafeteria at Novell that has been converted into a breakfast and lunch eatery opened to the public through a re-design of its brand identity. As the café offers meals made from scratch using fresh, quality ingredients, the new brand identity system was made fresh, modern and inviting.

chefBURGER

BUILDING BETTER BURGERS

ChefBURGER

design studio
Tad Carpenter Creative

design & in collaboration with
Design Ranch

design
Tad Carpenter

A collaboration between Tad Carpenter and Design Ranch
has resulted in the design ChefBURGER's visual identity
which expresses the build-your-own-burger concept of the
outlet. To convey that there are no set rules to making burgers,
a monster head was designed with ever-changing details.

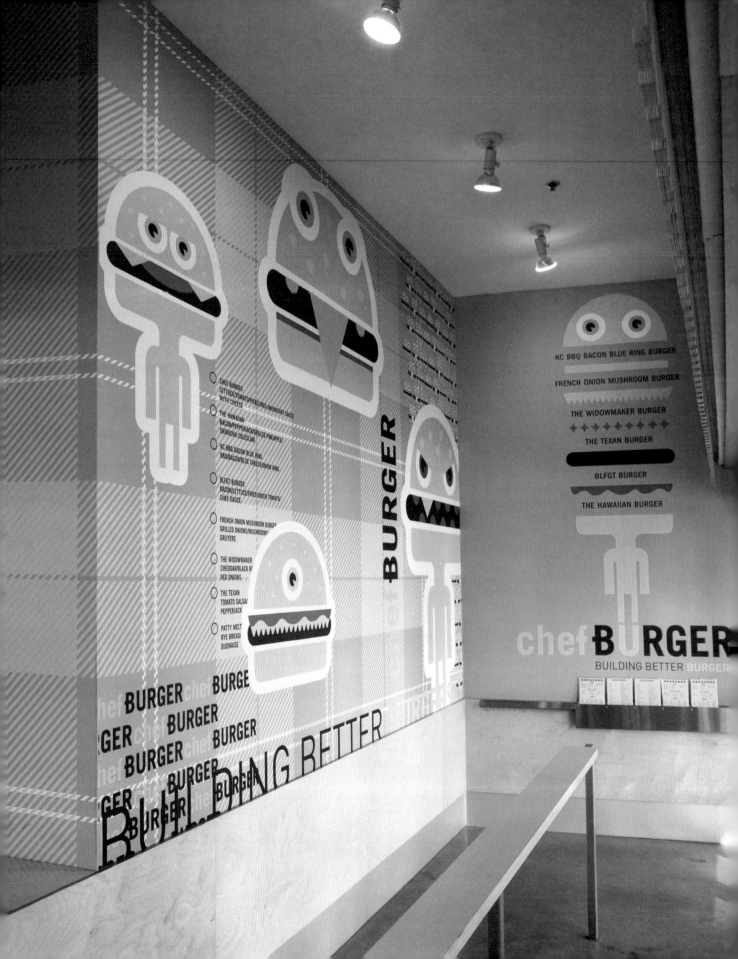

WWW.CHICKENPECKER.COM

Chicken Pecker

design studio
Commune

art direction
Ryo Ueda

design
Ryo Ueda, Minami Mabuchi, Natsumi Oguma,
Daisuke Takada, Yuji Terada, Kazuki Murata

photography
Tatsuo Kosukegawa, Hitoshi Yoneyama, Tsubasa Fujikura,
Kei Furuse [GAZEfotographica]

copywriting
Kosuke Ikehata

printing direction
Takaaki Tsukada

A chicken specialty restaurant, Chicken Pecker serves grilled
dishes, deep fried chicken, hamburgers, and rice bowls. Meticulous
in every aspect of preparation from ingredients and recipes, to safety
and service, this restaurant's simplicity and outstanding quality
lies in its passion. All visual elements such as the logo, signage
and menu were redesigned to reflect the charm of a Japanese
countryside restaurant that specialises simply in serving chicken.

41

すべてはここから。チキンペッカーの代名詞

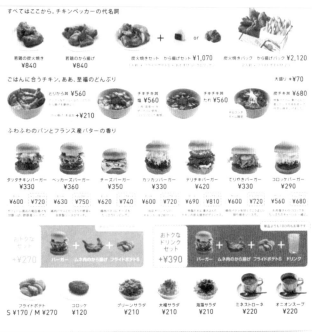

若鶏の炭火焼き ¥840 　若鶏のから揚げ ¥840 　炭火焼きセット から揚げセット ¥1,070 　炭火焼きパック から揚げパック ¥2,120

ごはんに合うチキン。ああ、至福のどんぶり　　　　大盛り +¥70

とりから丼 ¥560 　チキチキ丼 塩 ¥560 　チキチキ丼 たれ ¥560 　炭チキ丼 ¥680

+¥210

ふわふわのパンとフランス産バターの香り

タツタチキンバーガー ¥330 　ペッカーズバーガー ¥360 　チーズバーガー ¥350 　カツカツバーガー ¥330 　テリチキバーガー ¥420 　てりやきバーガー ¥330 　コロッケバーガー ¥290

¥600　¥720 　¥630　¥750 　¥620　¥740 　¥600　¥720 　¥690　¥810 　¥600　¥720 　¥560　¥680

おトクな セット +¥270

バーガー ＋ ムネ肉のから揚げ ＋ フライドポテトS

おトクな ドリンクセット +¥390

バーガー ＋ ムネ肉のから揚げ ＋ フライドポテトS ＋ ドリンク

フライドポテト S ¥170 / M ¥270 　コロッケ ¥120 　グリーンサラダ ¥210 　大根サラダ ¥210 　海藻サラダ ¥210 　ミネストローネ ¥220 　オニオンスープ ¥220

HOT DRINK

コーヒー　　　¥210
紅茶　　　　　¥190
ウーロン茶　　¥190

COLD DRINK

アイスコーヒー　¥210
ウーロン茶　　　¥190
ペプシコーラ　　¥190
レモンスカッシュ ¥190
オレンジジュース ¥190

アイスクリーム 各 ¥260

見た目だけが、ファストフード。

そう、チキンペッカーは、早さや効率を売りにはしていません。
ていねいに選んだ本物の素材を、ていねいな作り方で、本物の味に。
その違いは、一度食べればきっとわかってもらえると思っています。

01 素材がちがう。

チキンペッカーのチキンは有機農業の村、北海道中札内村産。3軒2農家で生産された若鶏が届きます。鶏の餌には不飽和な日モギ落葉なども使用。やわらかく、脂肪分が少ないうえに、臭みを抑えたコクのある美味しさが特長です。

02 安全がちがう。

実は、現在の養鶏では飼料に対する抗生物質の添加が不必要だなどです。チキンペッカーの契約農家では、その投薬をしない休薬期間を国の基準の3倍以上に設定し、一般に安全性を売りにしている鶏肉の2倍以上に設定している。そう安全性に配慮しています。

03 製法がちがう。

炭火焼きは「遠赤ならば」の優しい火で20〜30分かけて焼き上げます。その日の気温や湿度に合わせて火力の調節に気を使っています。から揚げは厳選した特製の若鶏油で揚げるので「サクッ」とした歯ざわりとあっさりとした風味が自慢です。

チキンの
おいしい
食べかた
専門店

CHICKEN PECKER

夢中でほうばる、無言でほうばる。

📞 テレフォンオーダー

お店に来る前に注文しておこう。

電話で予約注文 → ご来店 → できたてをお渡し！

0120-298-908

🛍 全国発送

店頭かウェブサイトにてご注文ください。

看板メニューである「若鶏の炭火焼き」「若鶏のから揚げ」を真空パックで発送します。

商品代金		送料			
3人前	¥2,520	北海道	¥750	中部	¥1,270
4人前	¥3,400	北東北	¥960	関西	¥1,480
5人前	¥4,250	南東北	¥1,060	四国	¥1,590
6人前	¥5,100	関東	¥1,170	九州	¥1,800
7人前	¥5,950	信越	¥1,170	沖縄	¥1,900
8人前	¥6,800	北陸	¥1,270		
9人前	¥7,650				
10人前	¥8,500				

CHICKEN PECKER

WWW.CHICKENPECKER.COM

チキンペッカー
〒004-0052
北海道札幌市厚別区厚別中央2条4丁目11-39
TEL 011-894-2989　FAX 011-894-1389
営業時間 10:00AM-8:00PM 年中無休

Le Buro

design studio
Inventaire

creative direction
Thomas Verdu, Estève Despond

design
Thomas Verdu, Estève Despond

Le Buro is a unique restaurant that marries clean architectural lines with early twentieth century elements. Hence, the design palette has adopted a warm and accessible hand-written logo. The restaurant's goal is to have the ability to attract a diverse clientele. To achieve this appeal, bold graphic lines were created using large typographic compositions that grabs attention and sparks curiosity easily. These compositions were also conceived as an element of decoration that gives the walls added depth and dynamism. Similar typographical compositions were also applied to the restaurant's range of informational and promotional materials such as menus and leaflets.

CULTURE

BEFORE-PARTY +28
LES DIAMANTS SONT ETERNELS

VE 12.09

OLIVER SAX, SAXOPHONISTE DE PARIS
AU BURO DES 19H00

SEASONTREE & DJ GUNTHERSTAXX AUX ARCHIVES DES 21H00
ENTREE GRATUITE

— BEFORE-PARTY —

CULTURE

GRAND CONCERT
AUX ARCHIVES (SOUS-SOL)

VE 5.09

PRIMASH AND THE DREAMS COLLECTER & DJ KAB

OUVERTURE DES PORTES 21H00
ENTREE GRATUITE

— CONCERT —

GIN FIZZ
FROZEN MARGARITA
CAIPI
RHUM PLANTER PUNCH
PINA COLADA
CAIPIROSKA

— COCKTAILS —

WHISKY
CHIVAS REGAL 18
RHUM
WYBOROWA EXQUISITE
FOUR ROSES
HAVANA CLUB

— ALCOOLS FORTS —

D stock gourmet

design studio
Estudio Eosméxico

design
Mauricio Lara and Sebastián Lara

in collaboration with
Ana Rodríguez, Joaquin Briseño, Francisco Rodríguez,
Darius Lau, Aldo Cancino, Cristina Aguilar

photography
Estudio Eosméxico, Pablo Fernández del Valle

A visual proposal based on the letter D for degustation, delicacy and delight was made for D Stock Gourmet store. The designers have come up with a neutral, black and white identity. Notable creative uses of the logo include the tiled floor manufactured by a Guadalajara workshop. It uses the letter 'D' as the main element in a geometric composition, recalling traditional Mexican tiles. The simplicity of the furniture with its bright white lacquer highlights the products in a space which has a domestic feel of homemade food. The consistency of the design covered the interiors, lighting, products, packaging, staff uniforms and other visual elements. Interesting facts about the Nayarit Riviera were also rubber stamped onto cards and bags. Highlighting the colours and textures of freshly-baked bread, salsas, tea boxes are traditionally hand-woven baskets. Ribbons with motifs similar to the tiles adorn the crepe paper used for the packaging.

Antoinette

design studio
Manic Design

photography
Zen Lee, Benjamin Koh

Manic Design undertook the crafting of the brand
identity and packaging for Antoinette, a French-inspired
brasserie and pâtisserie. The design work features the
chef's signature French style as well as elements of
contemporary re-interpretations of the classic style.

Brót Bakery

design studio
David Barath Design

photography
Daniel Vegel, David Barath

Brót Bakery produces handmade baked goods the traditional way
without preservatives or artificial colourings. Wanting to acclimatise
German delicacies in the Hungarian market, the owners named
the bakery Brót, which means bread in the German language.
In order to emphasise the natural and rustic sense of the brand,
the logo is shaped as a loaf of bread, making it easily decoded
and recognisable. The handwritten typeface is also placed on bags,
stationery, and packaging that are made using brown wrapping paper.

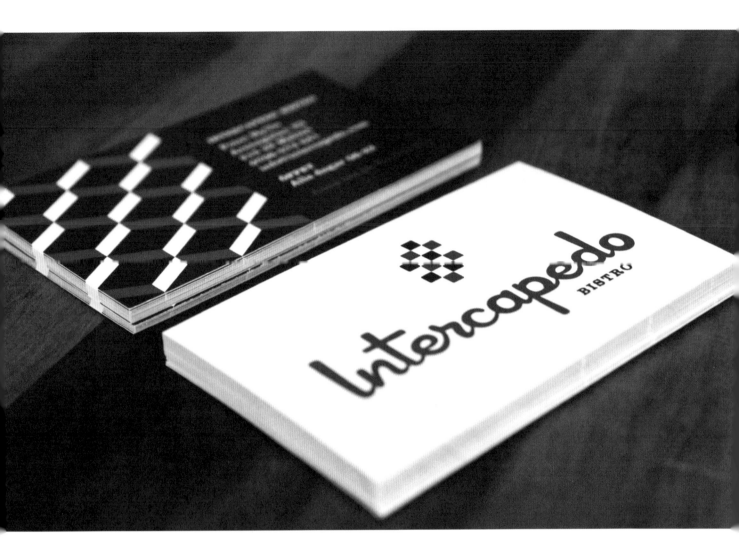

Intercapedo Bistro

design agency
Kollor Design Agency

photography
Kollor Design Agency

Opened in 2010, Intercapedo Bistro is located in the centre of Malmö,
Sweden, along the Hyllie district. In this district, the bistro provides
the commuters and nearby businesses with convenient breakfasts
or lunches. Intercapedo in Latin, means a break between two parts,
be it a concert or a game of sports. Similarly, this idea of taking
a break has been translated into its name card and food carriers,
exuding a cosmopolitan and modern feel for its busy patrons.

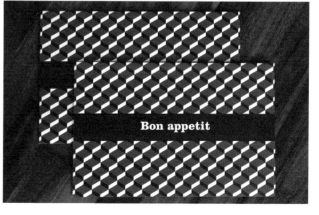

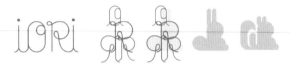

iori

design studio
Tea Time Studio

design
Sebastian Litmanovich

iori is a Japanese-styled hotel, restaurant and shop at Pirineos
Catalanes in Vielha City. For this particular project, Tea Time Studio
developed its global identity including the logo, icons, stationery,
pins, packaging, signage, gadgets, website and other visual
communication platforms. The image of the bunny was inspired
by a traditional Japanese image of "the rabbit in the moon" which
represents an occasion celebrated annually for prosperity. All icons
and illustrations were created based on the logo's typeface.

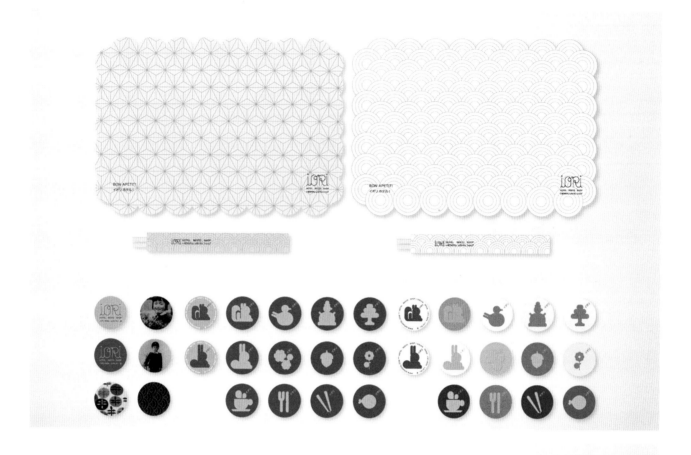

S1
TOKYO
東京スイート

HOMBRES
男

BAR
バー

DUCHA
シャワー

S2
OSAKA
大阪スイート

MUJERES
女

DESAYUNO
朝食

P
PARKING
駐車場

R1
SAKURA
桜ルーム

GUARDA ESQUI
スキールーム

COCINA
キッチン

H
HOTEL
ホテル

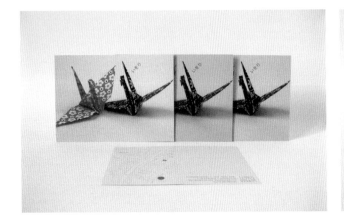

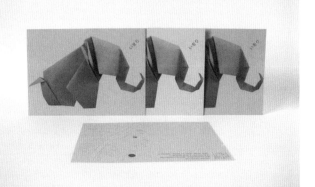

LA
CIGALA
ZUL

La Cigala Zul

design studio
Savvy Studio

La Cigala Zul is a brand new seafood restaurant located in an
area already saturated with dining places. In order to raise its
profile among the patrons of the area, a unique user experience
was achieved through the design of spaces, identity and other
communication elements that questioned what it was like to live
in a coastal city. This immediately built a connection with patrons.
Naval colours and symbols used around the restaurant and incorporated
into a menu that resemble port arrival documents and journals.
In addition, a hand-drawn typeface exudes the sense of nostalgia
with olden day registration numbers on the hull of ships and boats.

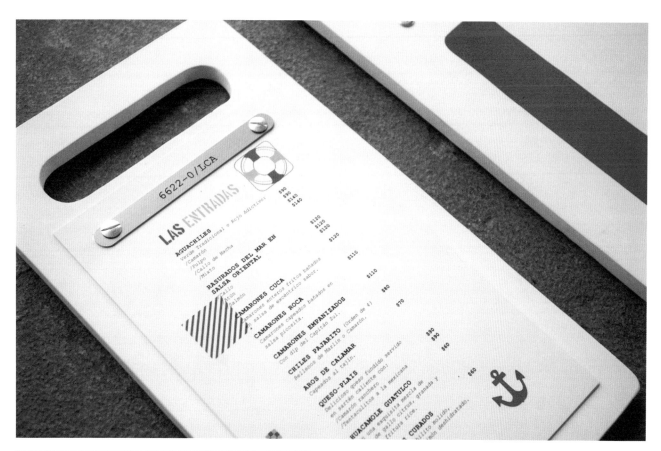

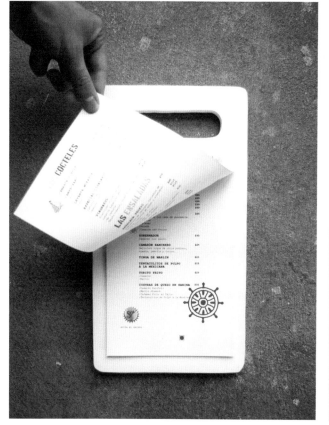

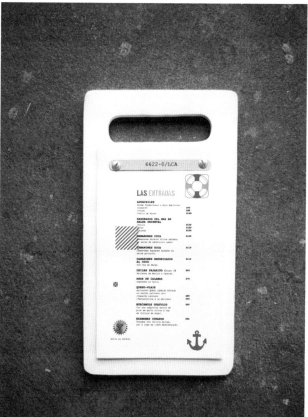

MARISQUERIA
SABROSA

LA
CIGALA
ZUL

L

MAT. N
6622-0

L A C I G A L A

A B C D E F G H
I J K L M N O P
Q R S T U V W X
Y Z 0 1 2 3 4 5
6 7 8 9

LA
CIGALA
ZUL

MARISQUERIA
SABROSA

RIO GRIJALVA 210, CENTRITO VALLE • T-8356-1333 • WWW.LACIGALAZUL.COM

COME COMO
CAPITÁN,
BEBE COMO
MARINERO

RIO GRIJALVA 210, CENTRITO VALLE • T-8356-1333
WWW.LACIGALAZUL.COM

LA
CIGALA
ZUL

Sláinte

design
Sam Jovana

Sláinte is a conceptual Scottish pub created for an academic project on visual identity. Set in Brazil, the need to be distinctively Scottish was paramount. Hence, the design intended to explore the irreverence, humour and wit of Scottish pub culture. A popular myth associated with Scotland is the Loch Ness monster, which designer Sam Jovana has drawn upon to create a typeface made of shapes resembling the creature. A symbol was created based on the revision of old Scottish beer bottle labels that often depict bearded men. The colour blue alludes to the sea surrounding Scotland, and orange represents the coastal stones when shone upon by the sun and warmth of the Scottish people—a colour palette that is both laid-back and uplifting. Characters and motifs typically representing Scottish culture were also designed with adapted popular Scottish aphorisms in addition to a graphic game for pub-goers.

sláinte

ALFABETO INSTITUCIONAL

black rose

a b c d e f g h i j k
l m n o p q r s t u v
w x y z
1 2 3 4 5 6 7 8 9 0
.,:;/˜]´[=~)(*&¨%$#@!"

Futura Hv BT

ABCDEFGHIJKLMNOPQRST
UVXWYZ
a b c d e f g h i j k
l m n o p q r s t u v
w x y z
1 2 3 4 5 6 7 8 9 0
.,:;/~]´[=-)[*&¨%$#@!"

Futura Lt BT

ABCDEFGHIJKLMNOPQRST
UVXWYZ
a b c d e f g h i j k
l m n o p q r s t u v
w x y z
1 2 3 4 5 6 7 8 9 0
.,:;/~]´[=-)[*&¨%$#@!"

rua pernambuco, 900
savassi ~ bhzte/mg.
(31) 8785 ~ 2379
iamdrunk@slainte.com

Frostbite

design studio
A Beautiful Design

Frostbite is a chain of shops selling gourmet popsicles. To avoid being mistaken for ice cream, the name Frostbite was coined and accompanied by the tag line "Since Ice Was Discovered". The logo is made up of popsicles that spell its name. The inspiration for the design was drawn from old American towns using traditional ice cream sticks, wood textures and a motif frame. Modern design additions include mascots, captions and colourful stickers.

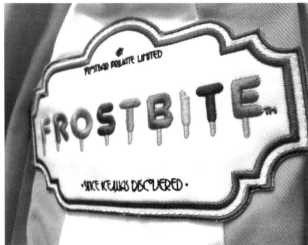

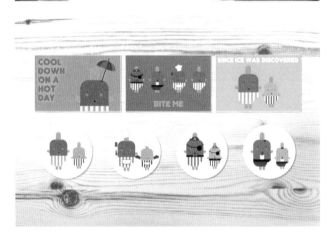

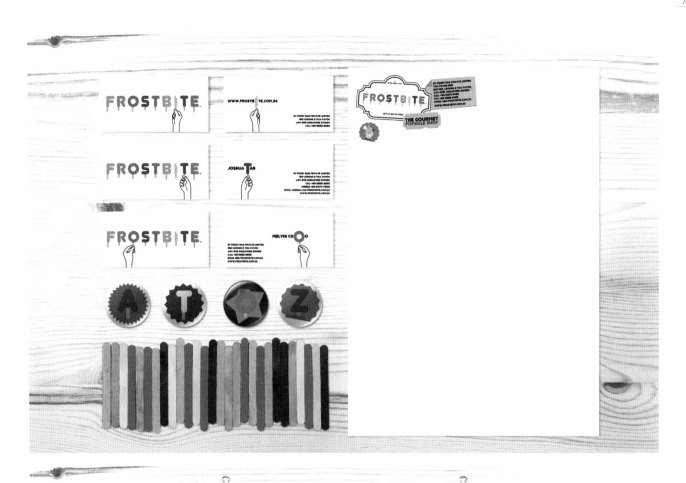

Costa Chica

design studio
Savvy Studio

The design concept of the seafood restaurant Costa Chica is closely related to its sister restaurant Costa Nueva, but adopts a more practical and simple approach. The visual language for Costa Chica draws from the freshness of ingredients, allowing diners to feel transported close to the coast. By applying graphic elements in smaller amounts and with restraint, they acquire greater importance within the visual composition, a direct analogy of the simplicity, freshness and practicality of Costa Chica.

COSTA CHICA

Glacé Artisan Ice Cream

design studio
Stir LLC

creative direction
Brent Anderson and Nathaniel Cooper

design
Nathaniel Cooper

photography
Gabe Hopkins

copywriting
Brent Anderson

Based in Kansas City, Glacé Artisan Ice Cream serves ice cream in fun and inventive flavours. Being under the same umbrella as Christopher Elbow Artisan Chocolates which locals are already familiar with, Glacé hopes to target the same audience. Although a clean, sophisticated and minimal visual identity was created for the brand, the copy and colour palettes ensure that it is still playful and approachable. The logo depicts melting drips of ice cream, suggestive of the tantalising ice cream flavours. Similar graphics were applied consistently across all consumer points of purchase in-store and online.

ICE CREAM

SMALL
1 TO 2 FLAVORS — $3.71

REGULAR
UP TO 3 FLAVORS — $4.76

ADD A SAUCE — $.50
• FLEUR DE SEL CARAMEL
• CHOCOLATE

AFFOGATO — $4.75
(SINGLE SERVING WITH ESPRESSO)

FRESH FRUIT FREEZE POPS — $1.50

HAND PACKED PINTS TO GO — $7.45

FLAVORS
THAI PEANUT CURRY
BANANAS FOSTER
BLUEBERRY CREAM CHEESE
STRAWBERRY THYME
GOAT CHEESE WITH WILDFLOWER HONEY
BLACKBERRY CHOCOLATE CHIP
KIWI SORBET
STRAWBERRY LIME SORBET
PINEAPPLE CILANTRO SORBET
CHOCOLATE SORBET
MANGO MINT SORBET

	12oz	16oz
	$1.75	$2.05
	$3.00	$3.50
	$3.50	$4.00
	$3.00	$3.50
	$2.00	$2.50
	$3.00	$3.50
	$2.00	$2.50
		$2.00
		$2.25
		$4.00
		$1.50
		$2.00

YOU'VE GOT GOOD TASTE

glacé
artisan ice cream

WHEN JOY FREEZES OVER

Costa Nueva

design studio
Savvy Studio

Costa Nueva is a seafood restaurant that offers the freshest ingredients from the pacific coast. Its prime location was a leverage upon which design studio Savvy wanted to convey in its visual identity: a casual and contemporary reinterpretation of the best food along the Mexican coast.

The main concept pays homage to the progressive and modern Mexico of the 1950s, also known as the "golden decade" for artists, architects and writers. The restaurant's slogan "Tan Lejos y Tan Cerca del Mar" (Far Away, Yet Close to the Sea) calls to mind the characteristic freshness of the ingredients served, juxtaposed against the luxury evoked by the interior design. The overall visual language is casual and relaxed, suggesting the simplicity of small traditional Mexican beach front eateries, contrasted with certain contemporary elements and vintage décor.

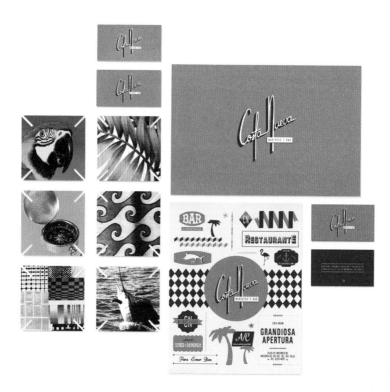

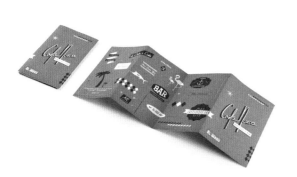

208 Duecento Otto

design studio
C Plus C Workshop Ltd

The first storey of this restaurant is a lively bar while the second storey is a tranquil dining area. Both floors offer al fresco dining with panoramic views of Hollywood Road. The logo design was based on the restaurant's address 208 and the outline of its door plate. Its visual identity was derived from the concept of mind maps, where the shapes and patterns formed by the people and food are connected. Artistically, it illustrates all the possibilities among the elements within the restaurant, creating an unforgettable trademark for the brand.

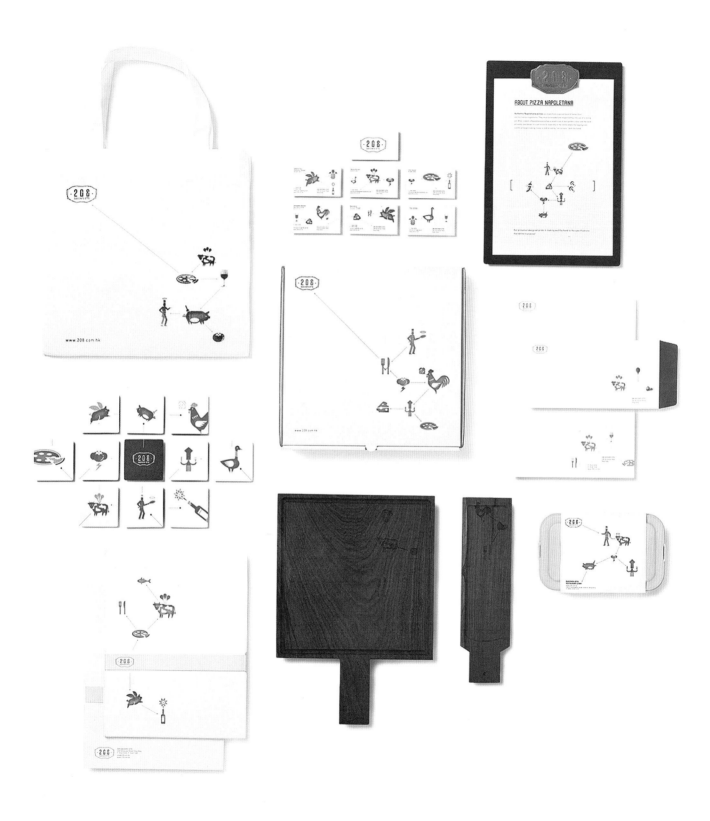

ZA NAPOLETANA

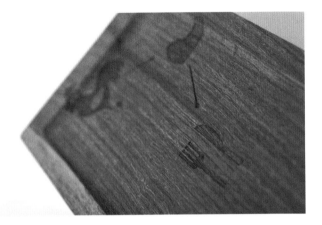

BAR ⋮ Please check in
at main entrance.

{Must be over twenty-one to imbibe}

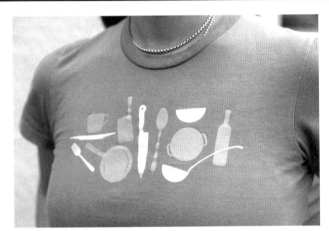

TAKE
ME
OUT.

juliankc.com

Julian

design studio
Stir LLC

creative direction
Brent Anderson

design
Nathaniel Cooper, Jordan Gray

photography
Gabe Hopkins

copywriting
Brent Anderson

The restaurant Julian features refined twists on familiar comfort foods whipped up by an award-winning chef, Celina Tio. The restaurant's name was derived from Tio's main cooking influences, Julia Child and her grandfather Julian. Design elements took cues from Child's kitchen which is known to be well-stocked, including her fondness for pegboards. Branding for the restaurant captures a familiar yet modern and fresh essence, bringing out the personality of its chef and how it would translate into its food and ambience.

Kongress Bar

design studio
Designliga

design
Andreas Döhring

photography
Designliga

Kongress Bar is located at the Congress Hall on the heritage-preserved premises of Munich's old exhibition centre, Alte Messe. The bar was designed by its owner, the Edith-Haberland-Wagner Foundation, to echo the 1950s style of the Congress Hall. The content and form of the central theme was inspired by the building that houses it and based on influences from German post-war boom year (Wirtschaftswunder). Its logo and communication material were shaped by the simple elegance and clean lines of the 1950s, creating an overall image in harmony with the building and the refined aesthetics of bar culture.

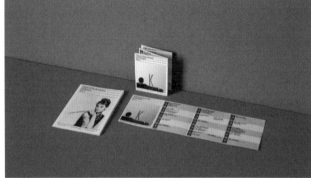

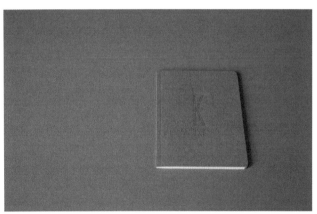

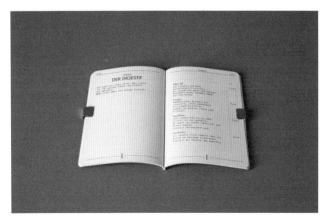

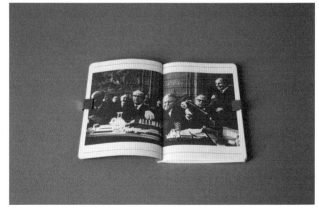

Krusta Bakery

design studio
Touch Branding

The identity of Czech artisan bakery, Krusta is a reflection of
the company's business strategy to follow old traditional recipes
but prepare them with the most modern techniques. That is why
the identity is based around old traditional handmade folk art but
executed with modern style and vector precision.

PanPan

design
Rocío Martinavarro

The visual identity for Spanish bakery PanPan is based on
a pattern that serves as a contemporary interpretation of an
ear of wheat—the main ingredient in bread. The result is a
simple and recognisable pattern reminiscent of antique artisan
techniques like weaving esparto baskets for displaying bread.
The concept behind the name PanPan (literally "BreadBread")
was derived using repetition in order to emphasise authenticity
and sincerity in understanding the vernacular love of bread.

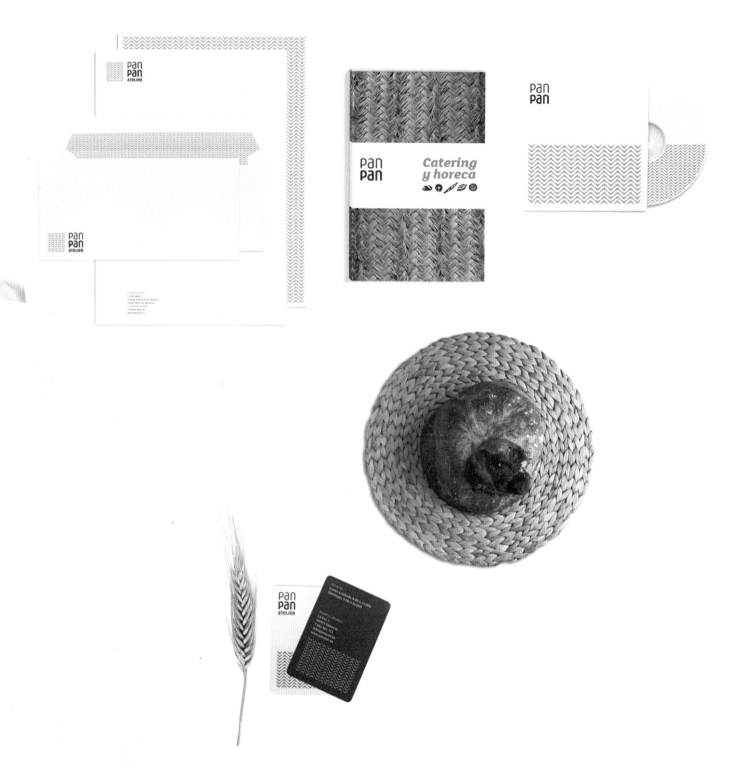

Lento leeento.
Sin prisas.
Así es el proceso
de elaboración del
auténtico pan.
PANPAN. Repetirás

Kichn

design studio
pupilpeople

Kichn is a concept café that has a unique customisable menu.
A series of taglines were crafted to shape the café's character
and the use of typography differentiates it from its competitors
who rely heavily on images. Keeping within budgets, all collateral
have been designed to be cost effective—A1-sized posters for its
opening were designed to be folded into takeaway food carriers.

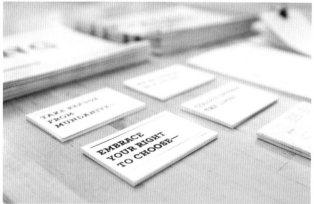

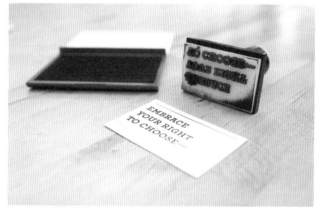

Why let us decide how your
Try bringing a little spontaneity ba
Sip a peachy green tea blend, have a dash
strawberry in that redbull mix or go wild and
concoct a lychee-milo-oreo blend (wow, we know),
and do keep a lookout for our featured special.
We embrace your right to choose—

EMBRACE YOUR RIGHT TO CHOOSE—

STRAWBERRY
MANGO
GREEN TEA
COFFEE
LYCHEE
REDBULL
FEATURED SPECIAL
GRAPE
PINEAPPLE
HONEY
MILO
CHOCOLATE
OREO

SINGLE BLEND— $4.90
DOUBLE BLEND— $5.90
TRIPLE BLEND— $6.90

in the ktchn.

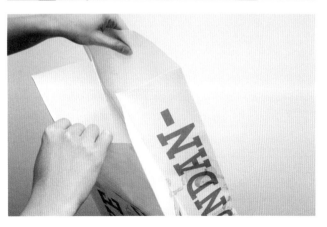

Marktachterl

design studio
Typejockeys

Marktachterl is a restaurant located on Karmelitermarkt in Vienna.
Its logo is derived from the existing neon lettering at its exterior.
Using the charm of this exterior signage, its logo is set against
a backdrop of nostalgic photos of a nearby market. This has been
applied to different surfaces such as rough paper, which juxtaposes
the soft emotions intended by the graphics.

The Pizza Makers

design studio
Smith & Milton

design & illustration
Ruth Pearson, Caroline Phillips, Dave Taylor,
Jasmine Spencer, Katie Pieczenko

photography
Andy Isaac

The concept behind The Pizza Makers is that they only make fresh
pizza, and not bake them. Hence, Pizzas can be delivered or taken
home to be baked at your own convenience. This very concept poses
a challenge for visual communication and branding as it deviates only
subtly from conventional pizza places. As problem solvers and thinkers,
Smith & Milton came up with the tagline "We Make, You Bake",
and stripped the overall look to a blackboard inspired visual language.
In doing so, they have achieved a style that is fresh and accessible,
allowing the skillfully handmade pizzas to speak for themselves.

GABBANI

1037 LVGANO

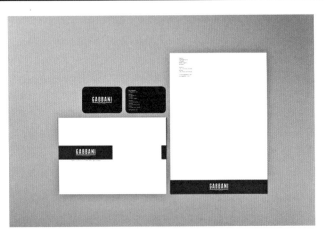

Gabbani

design studio
Demian Conrad Design

photography
Olivier Lovey, Sylvain Meltz

Established in 1937, Gabbani is the oldest delicatessen in the Italian-speaking region of Switzerland. The family business has survived, flourished and evolved into a synonymous name in the food industry. Creating a fashionable and bold identity was required for it to continue standing out amongst its competitors in the market. Visual references were made to the 1930s with a variety of typefaces, and from the 1960s with black-and-white optical art patterns.

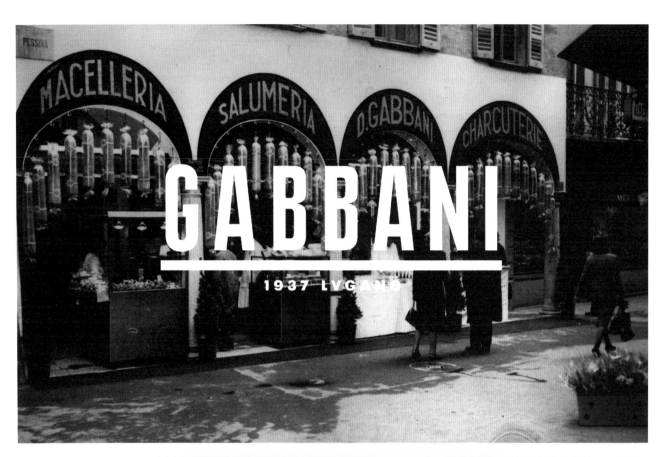

Mix n' Go

design agency
Kollor Design Agency

photography
Kollor Design Agency

Mix n' Go offers a new and unique dining concept with an array of fresh and healthy ingredients. Kollor Design wanted to express the central Stockholm restaurant's quality and innovation. They have done so using clean and crisp, but also warm and inviting design elements. Instead of simply applying pure dark grey to the logo, a touch of green has been blended into the colour treatment and instantly alludes to Mix n' Go's fresh ingredients. The logo's typeface has been partially redrawn, most apparently in the letter "G". The letters and the triangular symbol of the logo were used consistently on different mediums and platforms.

Just Green

design studio
BITE: Design

creative & art direction
Rex Ng

graphic design
Rex Ng

photography
Helen Sung

Just Green is a shop selling organic food products and goods.
In order to appear friendly, inviting and accessible, Bite Design
has created an easily recognisable icon system with a hand-drawn
typeface to add a sense of homemade goodness to its identity.

-DESDE 2010-
HORACIO
BARBATO

Horacio Barbato

design studio
Lip LTDA

creative direction
Lucho Correa

photography
Doping

illustration
Michael Halbert

This design intervention with Horacio Barbato began with the creation of its name, where it was discovered to be the same name borne by an ancient roman consul. Represented by a pig, its signage was intended to question about the pig's very identity and the name of the restaurant itself. This mysterious air surrounding the choice of its mascot creates distinct authenticity for the venue. The suggested image of Horacio Barbato also evokes lordship and a sense of centennial history that in turn, is contradicted by its rather recent opening in 2010.

New Wok

design studio
thisislove studio

design
Joana Areal

photography
thisislove studio

The conceptual development of the identity for the Asian fusion restaurant New Wok has resulted in a proposed game that can be played by diners. Its minimalism and expressiveness are express through technological plasticity, using the pixel as a primary design element.

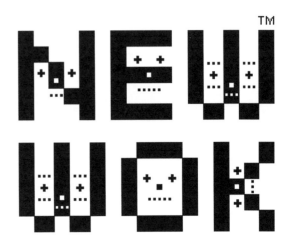

Market Lane Coffee

design studio
Swear Words

design
Scott Larritt, Sophie Good, Paul Greskie

photography
Tony Mott

stylist (photography)
Claire Larritt-Evans

architect
Deborah Lacey

Market Lane is a small, specialty micro-roaster and café located in Prahran Market, Melbourne. It sources and roasts specialty coffee from independent farms, estates and cooperatives. From brand-naming and in-store graphics through to the design and implementation of its website, the creative direction helmed by Swear Words enabled the chic Market Lane Coffee to gain a reputation for its carefully selected coffee beans and simplicity in design.

PARISH Foods & Goods

design studio
BoyBurnsBarn

Parish Foods & Goods is a New Orleans-inspired bi-level restaurant and market concept venue. It is located in a beautifully restored 1890s factory terminal building in the heart of Inman Park, Atlanta. The restaurant is defined by three concepts areas: Parish Restaurant, The Market at Parish, and To-Go at Parish. The eatery draws on French and Spanish influences that make New Orleans' cuisine and culture a melting pot of simple pleasures. Its comfortable casualness, good food and laid-back culture are what makes Parish Foods & Goods a choice destination for both local residents and visitors.

LuLu's

design studio
Stir LLC

creative direction
Brent Anderson

design
Sarah Nelsen

photography
Alistair Tutton

copywriting
Brent Anderson

With more that 10 years in operation, the expansion of Lulu's Thai Noodle Shop sees an opportunity to evolve its brand through design. Stir has managed to retain its fun and modern Asian appeal while reinventing its colour palette into fresher one. The vibrant colours selected were inspired by Thai food ingredients. Borrowing from traditional Thai imagery, icons and patterns were created to adorn booths, partitions and custom-made lamps. Outside, an illuminated signage draws attention from passers-by while a large wall facing the street has been converted into a billboard.

Gomez

design studio
Savvy Studio

The Gomez concept revolves around being a favourite global neighbourhood tavern amongst the San Pedro Garza García community. An identity that reflected the locals was needed to give the bar a friendly and fun graphic personality, appealing to a local and an international audience. To achieve this, Savvy developed playful iconography that conjures the Gomez concept, applying it to the interiors, menus and publicity materials. The icons represent a myriad of elements such as a music jukebox, casual food, cold beer, friendly bartenders, artisan mescal from Oaxaca, and most importantly, happy moments.

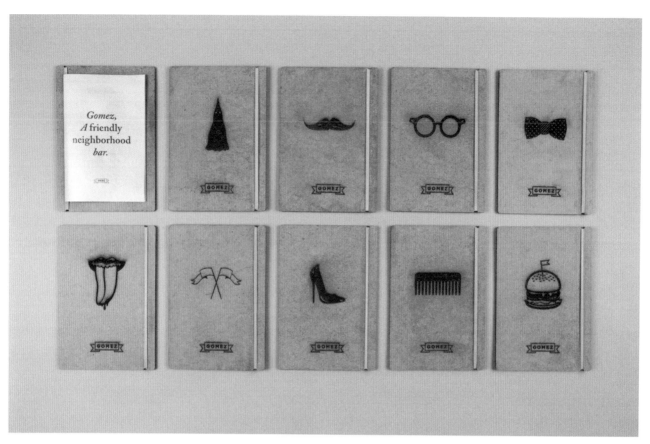

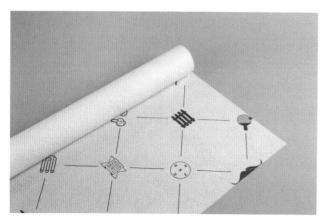

After-Office *Friendly.*

Yeah! Burger

design studio
Tad Carpenter Creative

design
Tad Carpenter

Yeah! Burger is a modern burger dining concept based on
sourcing local food and making healthy diet choices. It prides
itself on offering local meats, grains and food produced in
Atlanta-Georgia area. The extensive use of happy and bright
colours in its visual identity has been applied onto quirky
badges, through to the menu, t-shirts and other collateral.

YEAH! BURGER

BURGERS & MORE

All of our patties are made with organic or natural ingredients and are free of antibiotics, hormones and preservatives.
All of our meats are humanely-raised. Our burgers and sandwiches are always cooked fresh, right when you order!

① CHOOSE YOUR PATTY

BEEF BURGER	BISON BURGER	TURKEY BURGER	VEGGIE BURGER	GRILLED CHICKEN BREAST SANDWICH
A double stack of grass-fed, Georgia-raised beef	Colorado grass-fed bison	Certified organic turkey	Made with certified organic Sea Island red peas	Certified organic chicken
$6.99	$7.99	$5.99	$5.99	$5.99

② CHOOSE YOUR BUN

SOUTHERN WHITE	WHOLE WHEAT	GLUTEN-FREE WHITE	LETTUCE WRAP
Made with organic flour by H&F bakery	Made with organic flour by H&F bakery	Add $1.25	Green leaf lettuce

③ TOP IT OFF!

ADD CHEESE!
Certified organic cheeses
$1 EACH

AMERICAN   PEPPER JACK
BLUE   PIMENTO
CHEDDAR   SWISS

FREE TOPPINGS
(So far it!)

LETTUCE   CHOPPED VIDALIA ONIONS Organic
TOMATO   SLICED VIDALIA ONIONS Organic
DILL PICKLES   GRILLED VIDALIA ONIONS Organic
JALAPENOS   SUNFLOWER SPROUTS

PREMIUM TOPPINGS
$1 EACH

NITRATE-FREE BACON   SLICED AVOCADO
TURKEY BACON   NAPA COLESLAW
SAUTÉED MUSHROOMS
CAGE-FREE FRIED EGG Organic

④ GET SAUCED!

All sauces are FREE on your burger or sandwich! Try as a dipping sauce with fries for $.50 EACH

YEAH! SAUCE   HONEY MUSTARD   ROASTED GARLIC AIOLI   MISSISSIPPI MOP BBQ
KETCHUP   DUKE'S MAYO   BACON JAM   WHITE BBQ
MUSTARD   HOT ALABAMA RELISH   BLACK PEPPERCORN STEAK   ROOSTER SAUCE

HOT DOGS

Featuring Let's be Frank all-natural hot dogs!
Served on a Southern White bun made with organic flour

THE CLASSIC $4.99
Grass-fed beef hot dog with your choice of toppings from above

SOUTHERN DOG $5.99
Grass-fed beef hot dog topped with Pimento cheese, chopped
Vidalia onions and hot Alabama relish

CHILI & CHEESE DOG $5.99
Grass-fed beef hot dog topped with Shaun's red chili, organic
American cheese and jalapenos

SALADS

All of our salads are made with organic lettuce!

SIMPLE GREENS $5.99
Lettuce, cucumber, radish and fresh herb lemon vinaigrette
WITH GRILLED ORGANIC CHICKEN $9.99

CAESAR SALAD $5.99
Lettuce, croutons, Parmigiano cheese and Caesar dressing
WITH GRILLED ORGANIC CHICKEN $9.99

CLASSIC COBB $9.99
Lettuce, avocado, nitrate-free bacon, grilled organic
chicken, hardboiled egg, organic blue cheese crumbles
and Johnson Family Farms buttermilk ranch dressing

SIDES $2.49 EACH Add dipping sauces for $.50!

We use 100% heart-healthy canola oil for our fries, onion
rings and pickles!

HAND-CUT FRENCH FRIES	FRIED PICKLES
GLUTEN-FREE FRENCH FRIES	KETTLE POTATO CHIPS $1.49
BUTTERMILK VIDALIA ONION RINGS	CUP OF SHAUN'S RED CHILI
FIFTY-FIFTY	CUP OF NAPA COLESLAW
Half French fries, half onion rings	

KIDDIE COMBOS

All Kiddie Combos come with french fries, choice
of an organic milk box or organic apple juice

BURGER COMBO $6.99
Single patty grass-fed beef burger

HOT DOG COMBO $6.99
Grass-fed beef hot dog

ICE CREAM
Featuring Strauss Family Creamery organic soft-serve ice cream!

MILK SHAKES
Made with certified organic milk!
$4.99 EACH

CHOCOLATE
VANILLA
STRAWBERRY
PEACH
COFFEE
COOKIES AND CREAM
WHYNATTE

FLOATS
Featuring Boylan sodas with 100% cane sugar
$4.99 EACH

BROWN COW
Vanilla ice cream with Root Beer
BLACK COW
Vanilla ice cream with Black Cherry soda
CREAMSICLE
Vanilla ice cream with Orange soda

CONCRETES $4.99 EACH
Vanilla soft-serve ice cream blended at high speed with your favorite mix-ins!
Your first mix-in is free! Add more for $.50 EACH.

MIX-INS
HOT FUDGE   CHOPPED PEANUTS   CHOCOLATE ALMOND BARK
COOKIES AND CREAM PEANUT BRITTLE   CHOCOLATE ESPRESSO BEANS
PEANUT BUTTER CUPS HEATH CANDY BAR

SUNDAES $4.99 EACH
Your choice of CHOCOLATE or VANILLA soft-serve ice cream in a cup with HOT FUDGE,
CHOPPED PEANUTS and FRESH WHIPPED CREAM

CUPS $2.99 EACH
Your choice of CHOCOLATE or VANILLA soft-serve ice cream

BEVERAGES
Alcoholic

BEER

DRAFTS	GLASS	PITCHER
BROWN LAGER Brooklyn Brewery	$5	$18
DOPPELBOCK Spaten Optimator	$5	$18
INDIA PALE ALE Harpoon	$5	$18
PALE ALE Sweetwater 420	$5	$18
TRIPEL ALE Chimay White	$8	$30

BOTTLES & CANS

INDIA PALE ALE Bass IPA Organic	$5
LAGER Pabst Blue Ribbon	$3
LAGER Budweiser	$3
LIGHT LAGER Bud Light	$3
LIGHT LAGER Amstel Light	$3
PALE LAGER Stella Artois	$5
GLUTEN-FREE Green's Amber Ale	$4

WINE

RED WINES

CABERNET SAUVIGNON Louis-Fitch, Sonoma '08	$5
MALBEC Yellow+Blue, Argentina '09 Organic	$6
PINOT NOIR Wild Hog, Russian River Valley '08	$8
SYRAH Qupé, Central California Coast '07	$12

WHITE WINES

CHARDONNAY Estancia, Monterey County '08	$6
PINOT GRIGIO Casa Delta, Italy '08	$6
ROSÉ Domaine de Nizas, France '08	$8
SAUVIGNON BLANC Yellow+Blue, Chile '08 Organic	$6

SIGNATURE COCKTAILS

MARGARITA Corazontador tequila, triple sec, lime and Hawaiian sea salt	$8
MOJITO Cruzan rum, muddled mint and lime	$8
FROZEN STRAWBERRY DAIQUIRI Rum, strawberries, lemon and ice	$8
RUBY RED EYE Absolut Ruby Red vodka, Campari and fresh grapefruit juice	$8
CRITICAL MASS Tuaca liqueur, Chimay White base and fresh orange juice	$9
COMSTOCK MULE High West Silver whiskey, ginger beer and lime	$9
DARK & STORMY Gosling's Black Rum, ginger beer and lime	$9
FATHER'S OFFICE Johnnie Walker Red whiskey, Cherry Heering, fresh orange juice	$9
RYE TOAST Old Overholt Rye whiskey, Cynar liqueur and lemon bitters	$9
MANHATTAN Russell's Reserve Rye, sweet vermouth and bitters	$9

BEVERAGES
Non-Alcoholic

SODA

DRAFTS	$1.75
Featuring Coca-Cola products	
COKE	
DIET COKE	
COKE ZERO	
SPRITE	
MELLOW YELLOW	
DR. PEPPER	
BARQ'S ROOT BEER	
BOTTLES	$3
Boylan sodas made with 100% cane sugar	
ROOT BEER	
ORANGE	
CREAM	
BLACK CHERRY	

TEA

BREWED	$1.75
Revolution Tea iced tea	
SWEET TEA	
UNSWEETENED TEA	
BOTTLED	$3
GREEN TEA Organic	

OTHER DRINKS

JUICES	
ORANGE JUICE Fresh-squeezed	$3
GRAPEFRUIT JUICE Fresh-squeezed	$3
ORGANIC APPLE JUICE POUCH	$2
SPARKLING BEVERAGES	$3
IZZE Clementine	
IZZE Peach	
ENERGY DRINKS	
RED BULL	$3.50
RED BULL SUGAR-FREE	$3.50
WHYNATTE	$3.25
VITAMIN WATER	
LEMONADE Multi-V	
ORANGE Essential	
TROPICAL CITRUS Energy	
WATER	
FILTERED WATER	FREE
BOTTLED WATER FIJI	$1.75
SPARKLING WATER San Pellegrino	$3
MILK	$3
Horizon organic milk boxes	
CHOCOLATE	
STRAWBERRY	
WHITE	

SPIRITS

GIN	
GORDON'S	$7
BEEFEATER	$8

RUM	
CAPTAIN MORGAN	$7
CRUZAN	$7
HORNE SPICED RUM	$7
GOSLING'S BLACK RUM	$8

TEQUILA	
CONQUISTADOR	$7
PATRON SILVER	$10

VODKA	
PRAIRIE ORGANIC	$7
GREY GOOSE	$9
BELVEDERE	$10

WHISKIES	
OLD OVERHOLT	$6
EVAN WILLIAMS	$7
FOUR ROSES SM. BATCH	$7
JACK DANIEL'S	$8
JAMESON	$8
JOHNNIE WALKER RED	$8
RUSSELL'S RESERVE RYE	$8
BASIL HAYDEN'S	$9
MAKER'S MARK	$9
HIGH WEST SILVER	$10
HIGH WEST RENDEZVOUS	$10
WOODFORD RESERVE	$10

1168 Howell Mill Road | Suite K
Atlanta, Georgia | 30318
P 404.496.4393 | F 404.496.4368
facebook.com/yeahburger | twitter.com/yeahburger

YEAHBURGER.COM

ERIK MAIER
MANAGING PARTNER
erik@yeahburger.com

1168 Howell Mill Road | Suite E | Atlanta, Georgia | 30318
P 404.496.4393 | F 404.496.4968 | M 404.386.3561
facebook.com/yeahburger | twitter.com/yeahburger

YEAHBURGER.COM

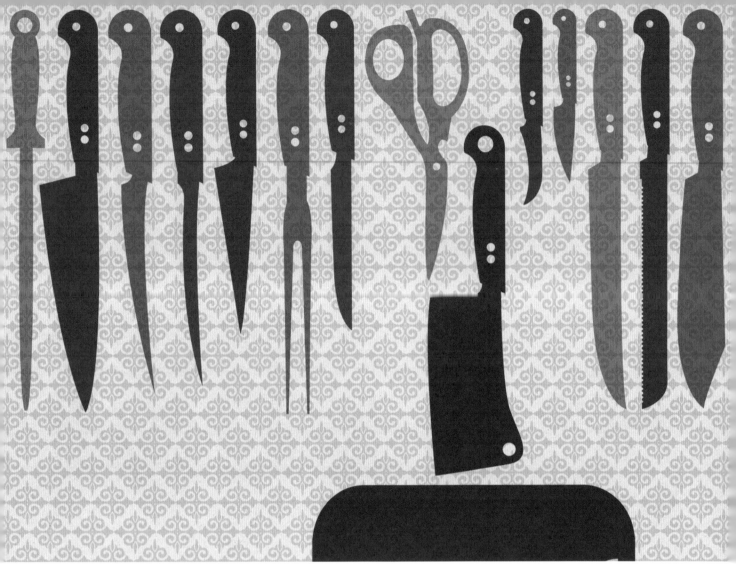

Mourella Restaurant

design studio
Meandyoucreative

This project involved the complete branding for a restaurant
situated by an idyllic beach on the island of Rhodes in Greece.
The idea of Greek tradition was re-interpreted through
the use of recycled paper and earthy tones blended with
modern and stylised illustrations. The logo for the restaurant
was created using the silhouettes of different types of
kitchen utensils with the frying pan as the main motif.

μούρελλα
φαγοπότι

Mundo Verde

design studio
Wallnut Studio

design
Cristina Londoño

photography
Alfonso Posada

Mundo Verde is a restaurant that serves salads and sandwiches,
and is committed to developing the freshest and healthiest foods.
Inspired by this, a highly typographical design identity was developed
to create an array of textures, wrapping papers and wall graphics
in which recipes, health recommendations and tips are featured.

PASIÓN
mousse preparado con chocolate blanco
y negro sobre confitura de moras

$5.500

Three Sixty

design studio
BoyBurnsBarn

Three Sixty is a restaurant that sits on top of Hilton Hotel overlooking key landmarks such as the Gateway Arch and Busch Stadium. Its roof on the 26th storey offers a 360° panoramic view of the city with a chef-driven menu and a full bar. The designers for this project's branding and collateral materials were asked to create an all encompassing logo with the numbers '3', '6' and '0' interlocked. Other collateral created include a powder coated steel tent-like menu with the logo water die-cut and placed on each table. The menu stand also doubles as a magnetic board to prevent order sheets and cheques from the natural elements associated with the restaurant's altitude. When placed on the menu stand facing north, the restaurant's name card also navigates the city's major land marks.

Stand

design studio
Base

Stand is a gourmet burger restaurant in New York City which Base Design has created a visual identity for. Its identity incorporates playful text into the logo itself and in other applications such as the interior and exterior signage, environment, promotional materials, print advertising, menus, packaging, staff uniforms, and merchandise. The particular typeface was selected for its "meaty" appearance, with two variations created to resemble the form of a burger.

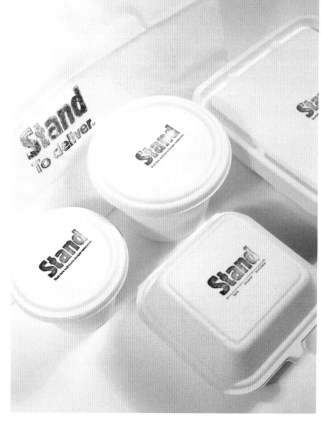

Stand

These days a well-done burger is rare.
**But a well-done burger is
not necessarily done well,
and a rare burger is not
necessarily well done.**
Stand is that rare burger restaurant where
everything is done well.

Medium

Stand

24 East 12th St. NYC
Tel. 212 488 5900

24 East 12th St. NYC
Tel. 212 488 5900

I me

name

gender

number

at Stand

Stand
That rare well-done burger restaurant.

**24 East 12th Street
New York NY 10003
Tel 212 488 5900**
www.standburger.com
To stay. To go. To deliver.

Star

These days a well-done
**But a well done
not necessarily
and a rare burg
necessarily we**
Introducing Stand, that rare well-do

Stand

That rare well-done burger restaurant.

quality solution. Safe and gentle on skin.
Use it to clean up or freshen up.

**Made by hand.
Eaten by hand.**

er is rare.

rger is

e well

is not

done.

er restaurant.

THE
COMMONS
LOCAL EATING HOUSE

The Commons

design studio
Craig & Karl

photography
Maja Baska

Branding and interior elements for The Commons - Local Eating House, a restaurant and bar located in the quiet backstreet of Darlinghurst, Sydney, Australia. The identity reflects the restaurant's slow and simple approach to dining with a reverence for local, seasonal produce.

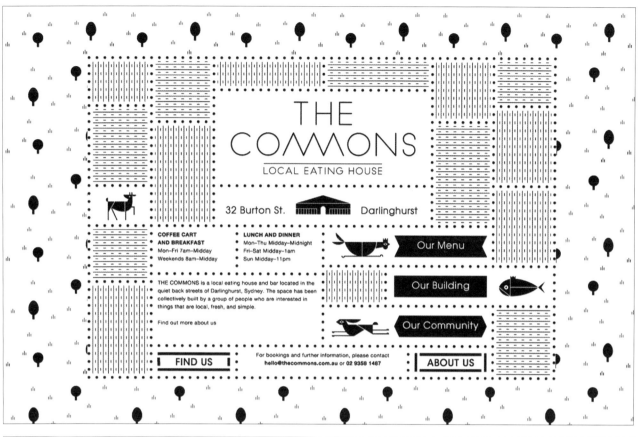

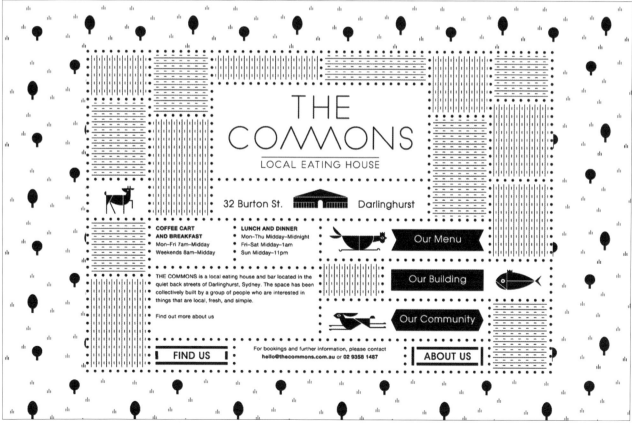

Pizzabella

creative direction
Tad Carpenter Creative

design & in collaboration with
Design Ranch

design
Tad Carpenter

Pizzabella is a pizza place that serves up pizzas baked with
an authentic wood-fired oven and non-traditional antipastos
such as bacon wrapped brussels sprouts and baked calamari
salad. The design identity for this pizza outlet aimed to convey
its contemporary interpretation of the traditional pizzeria.

Tap

design studio
BoyBurnsBarn

Tap is Atlanta's first gastropub. While it serves seasonal
and innovative comfort foods, its name draws upon the
restaurant's extensive draft beer and barrel wine selection.

The collateral designed for the restaurant encapsulates the
environment of a great community pub by being conversation
topics unto themselves. For example, the menu also serves as
a tour guide with a 'Beer Flavour Wheel' at the back while coasters
offer fun and interesting trivia for those waiting for their food to
be served. The intention of this design was to have each element
engaging the diner, creating a bond between them and the
dining space.

The Europa Café

design
Camila Drozd

The Europa Café is a small and charming shop located
on Main Street in Stroudsburg PA, offering a wide range
of European delicacies. The shop's logo, signage and
packaging were redesigned as a proposal to its owners
as a better reflection of the style and feel of the café.

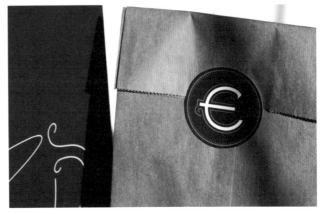

Pomms'

design studio
Motifs Concept & Design

design
Elke Kunneman, Sake van den Brule

illustration
Typex

The award-winning (Cannes Golden Lion, European Design Award)
visual identity for the Dutch food stand Pomms' was developed by
reputed multidisciplinary design agency Motifs. Taking into account what
Pomms' stands for, healthy snacks and responsible entrepreneurship,
Motifs consciously steered away from eco-clichéd marketing and
design. Instead, the focus was shifted to the appeal of delightfulness
and authenticity. The unique illustration plays a leading part in reflecting
Pomms' cradle-to-cradle approach; from its ingredients and authentic
recipes up to the sensible imps that dutifully clean up the mess.

Pomms'
de lekkerste van het land!

Maasstraat 119III
1078 HH Amsterdam
m: +31 (0)6 811 673 19
e: eetsmakelijk@pomms.nl

Over Pomms' Mobiele verkoopunit 100% Biologisch De oprichters

Pomms' Friet

Boer Jan uit de **Flevopolder** heeft de beste piepers voor ons uitgezocht op zijn akkers. Wij bakken ze **vers gesneden** in de schil voor de lekkerste smaak.

100% Biologisch Pomms'

Over Pomms'

Pomms' streeft ernaar om de allerlekkerste snacks te maken, iedere dag weer. Dit doen we volgens authentiek recept uit grootmoeders tijd. Bij het eten van een Pomms' kroket proef je biologisch rundvlees. En onze verse zelfgemaakte friet smaakt zoals ie moet smaken, naar aardappel. Maar Pomms' staat voor veel meer dan lekker eten. We bieden iedereen een gezonder alternatief. Gezond betekent bij Pomms' niet alleen minder vet meer vezels of vers fruit. Gezond staat ook voor gezond verstand. Zo onderneemt Pomms' diervriendelijk en gebruiken

Pomms' Mobiele verkoopunit

Publieke evenementen of een zakelijke bijeenkomst, in de openlucht of toch binnen. De mobiele verkoopunit van Pomms' is overal inzetbaar dankzij een revolutionair luchtzuiveringssysteem...

Pomms' 100% Biologische producten

Aardappelkenner Ron

De consument van nu wordt kritischer en kiest bewust voor gezondere voeding met verantwoorde herkomst. Het assortiment van Pomms' sluit hierop aan......

Pomms' Werken bij Pomms'

Pomms' is altijd op zoek naar leuke, enthousiaste mensen die willen helpen op evenementen en festivals zoals de Nijmeegse 4-daagse of Mysteryland. Heb je zin om het Pomms' team te versterken...

Pomms' Agenda

28 oktober
Festival van de duurzaamheid - Amsterdam

----

02 november t/m 05 november
Herfst carnaval - Rotterdam

----

08 november
Groenfest - Eindhoven

----

09 november
HISWA - RAi Amsterdam

Meer evenementen...

Table Nº1

design studio
Foreign Policy Design Group

brand direction
Arthur Chin

creative & art direction
Yah-Leng Yu

design
Tianyu Isaiah Zheng (TY)

Table Nº1 is Shanghai's first gastrobar that serves modern tapas-style European cuisine. It is set in a sleek and simplistic interior which encourages social interaction by sharing portions over a long communal table. Hence, the brand identity focuses on communal dining in a simple and unpretentious environment. This comes through from the use of brown craft paper and newsprint paper throughout the collateral system. Taking inspiration from the long communal tables, the business card is designed to be folded into a miniature table. Basic folders with clips are used for the menu while distressed and rusted clips align with the location's history as a former warehouse. In addition, order pads from newsprint paper are hand stamped with the logo.

Aschan Deli

design studio
Bond Creative Agency Oy

design
Aleksi Hautamäki, Tuukka Koivisto & Janne Norokytö

photography
Paavo Lehtonen

Aschan Deli is an urban quick-stop for breakfast, lunch, snacks or coffee. The aim of Bond was to design a concept that looks fresh, modern and convenient. Iconic food and beverage symbols used in the signage, interiors and collateral act as easy visual communicators and are a major element in the deli's visual identity. Bright colours were also introduced to bring more life and vibrance into the interior.

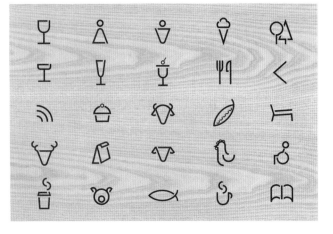

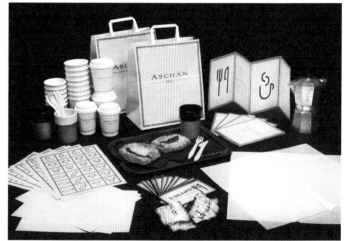

moomah

moomah

moomah

Moomah

design studio
Apartment One

The vision for Moomah was to be a space that encourages creativity, connection and imagination between parents, caregivers, children and friends. To create a new visual language that conveyed Moomah's four core values (connect, create, discover, nourish), three different variations of the M logo were created with elements that visually presented those values. By creating custom application-specific illustrations for particular objects such as stationary, cups, bags and stickers, the designers have crafted for Moomah a memorable and recognisable brand without having to put the same logo on every object and place.

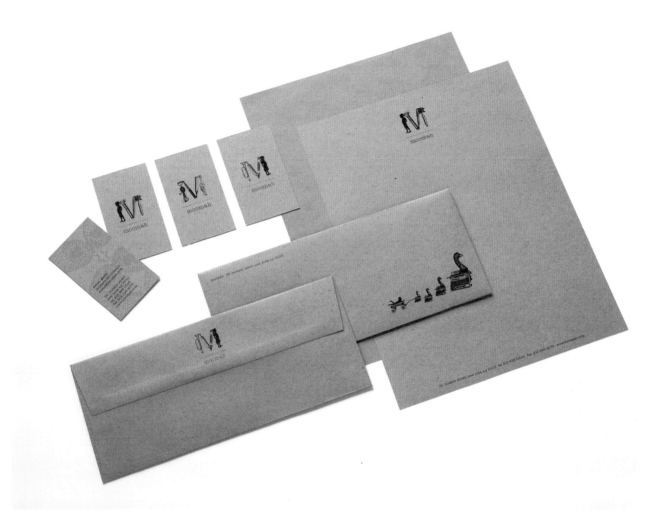

Platform

design studio
Subtrakt

design
Claire Hartley

photography
Yusuf Ozkizil Photography

Platform is a bar and restaurant that sits on the archway under the
London Bridge. Its interiors were designed by Sampson Associates,
while its visual identity such as in-house graphics, marketing collateral
and signage were designed by Substrakt.

Sweet Treat

design studio
Re-public

design
Stina Nordquist

photography
Re-public

Sweet Treat is a small coffee shop that focuses on quality coffee and excellent service. The simple and type-based logo exudes both a sense of good quality and courtesy. The negative spaces formed between the letters are significant as a reference to the idea of a pause—the time taken out from busy schedules and activities to visit the café, as well as the memorable moment of pleasure experienced when tasting something of superb quality.

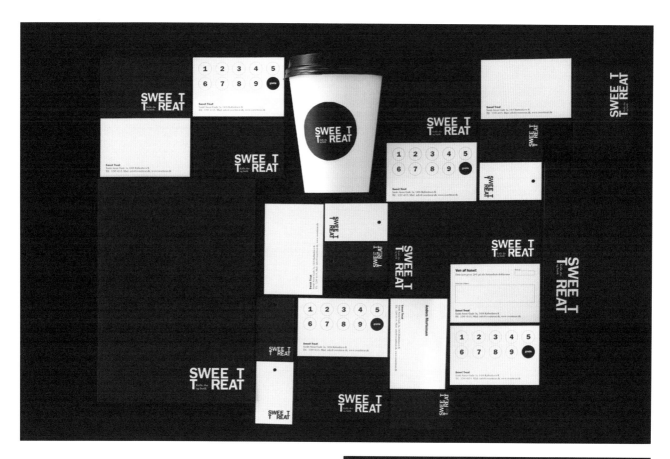

SWEE T
T REAT

Kaffe, the
og butik

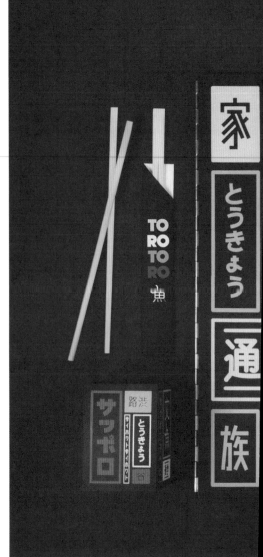

Toro Toro

design studio
Savvy Studio

Being a popular choice of cuisine in Monterrey, Japanese food is often served in fast food outlets, high-end restaurants or chain restaurants. Though gastronomic experiences in such places are varied and interesting, it also contributes to the formation of clichéd Asian aesthetics like pseudo Zen elements, and red and white plates. More than a just Japanese restaurant, Torotoro has been designed to transport diners to the heart of Tokyo by exploring its visual culture, vibrancy and dynamism. Neon lights and common symbols that inspire the sensation of being in an unfamiliar place, and an over-saturation of key visual elements of the Ginza commercial district, work to achieve a typical and authentic Japanese dining ambience.

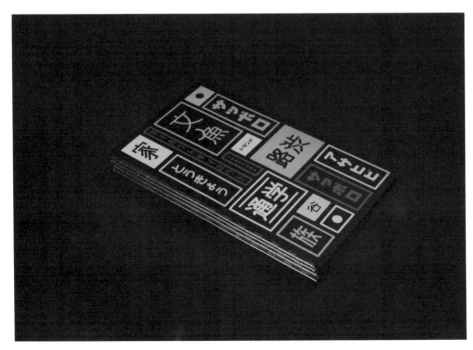

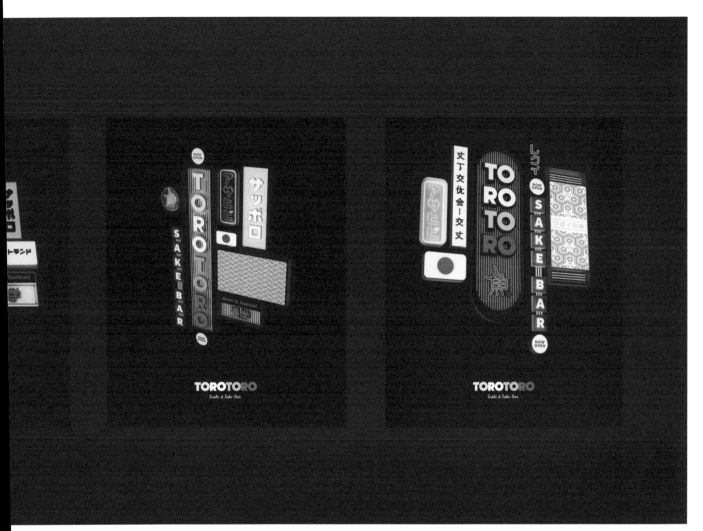

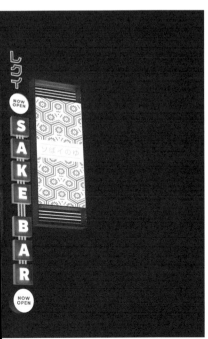

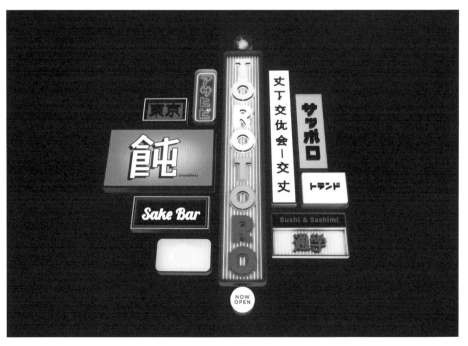

Txoko

design studio
LoSiento

design
Borja Martinez

photography
Jose Luis Lopez De Zubiria

The following graphic identity and packaging designs are for the Italian pasta restaurant, Txoko. The overall art direction of the visual identity articulates the restaurant's new fast food concept developed by Martín Berasategui. The main idea was to visually express the concept of quick change and adaptation in a logo that easily translates into different messages for collateral while still referring to the main Txoko name. In addition, this suggestion of food disappearing rapidly through photographs also comments on the deliciousness of the dishes served.

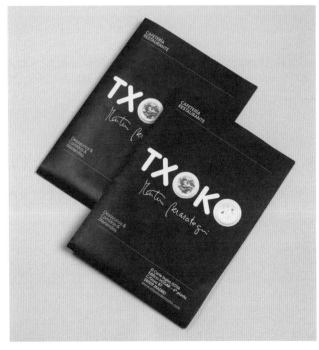

José Leos

design studio
Savvy Studio

Professionalism and attention to detail characterises the catering service of Chef José Leos, setting it ahead of industry counterparts. Maximising this advantage, the caterer's visual identity consists of graphic compositions where order, symmetry and a monochromatic palette reflect important aspects of professional catering: elegance, order, aesthetics and cleanliness. By applying its unique custom designed icons onto its various marketing platforms and points of purchase, José Leos immediately communicates the differentiated service it provides.

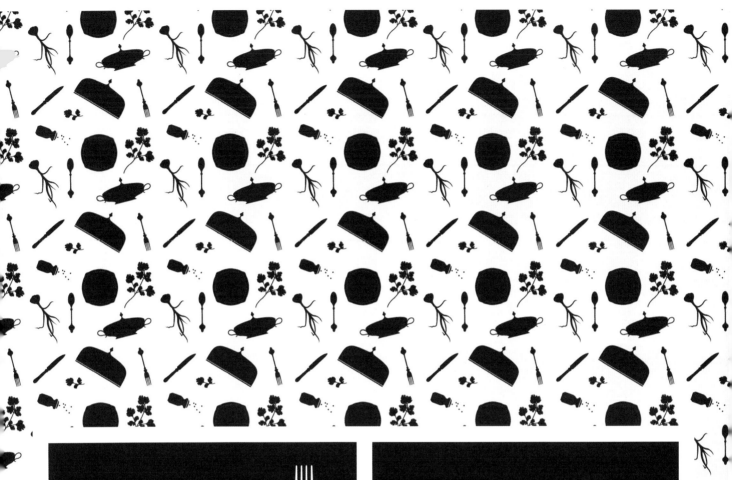

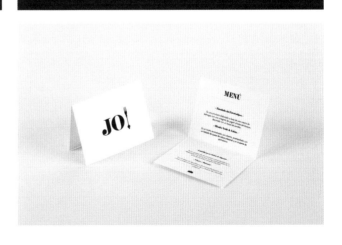

The Glass House

design
Catherine Bourdon

photography
The Glass House

The Glass House is a restaurant, bar and entertainment
venue that specialises in homemade beers, tasty snacks
and live music. Consisting mainly of seasonal menus and live
show flyers, this single colour identity allows for cost-effective
reproduction of restaurant paraphernalia and instant recognition
by diners and patrons. By infusing slight grit and copy machine
imperfections, the overall simple and sleek aesthetics of the
design is juxtaposed pleasantly. This gives the necessary tension
and flavour befitting the bar's punk and hard-core roots.

White wine
bottle/glass

25/7	Oveja Negra Chardonnay/Viognier Casablanca, Chile 2004
30/8	Domaines Felines-Jourdan Picpoul de Pinet Southern France 2004
30/8	Dr Loosen Blue Slate Riesling Mosel, Germany 2003
32	Knappstein Three Riesling Clare Valley, Australia 2004
40	D'Arenberg The Money Spider Roussanne McLaren Vale, Australia 2004
48	Alexia Sauvignon Blanc Nelson, New Zealand, 2004
53	Benefizium Porer Pinot Grigio Alois Lageder Alto Adige, Italy 2003
70	Catena Alta Chardonnay Mendoza Argentina 2002

The Vegetable Bar

design studio
Magpie Studio

creative direction
David Azurdia, Ben Christie, Jamie Ellul

design
David Azurdia

Springing up after the vegetable market closes every evening,
this impromptu venue is known to locals as The Vegetable Bar.
Its visual identity captures its nightly metamorphosis with a
vegetable/wine glass silhouette, and a subdued colour palette.

The Vegetable Bar
Fizz

The Vegetable Bar
Beer

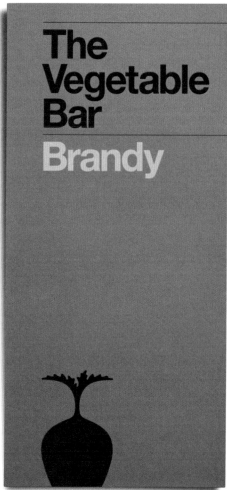

The Vegetable Bar
Brandy

thalle
-Strasse
g
43 3155

The Vegetable Bar

The Hummingbird

studio
Analogue

creative direction
Barry Darnell

design
Tez Humpreys

photography
Rob Booker

The Hummingbird is a three-storey restaurant and bar located in a small village in Leeds, the UK. It serves cuisine prepared with local produce and cocktails. With a design brief that spelled friendly, homely, relaxed and inviting, the designers adopted the restaurant's unique menu (changed daily based on availability of produce) as an inspiration for the design.

To bring out the tactility of the menu and other paraphernalia, special focus was given to using different textures and typography: menus were presented in handmade and distressed clip boards with 100% natural paper which gives its character through the visible impurities and fibres. The art direction for the food photography was also a key element in creating the right brand image: the logo is a mix of traditional and contemporary elements and the door sign had been deliberately fabricated in mild steel which will rust over time.

2-4-1
on Large Coffees

Simply present this voucher to receive 2 large coffees for the price of 1.
Offer valid monday to friday 8.30am until 11.30am & 2pm until 4pm. Valid until 30th September 2011.
Cannot be used in Conjunction with any other offer

The HUMMINGBIRD
HAPPY Hour
GREAT DEALS
ON SPECIAL SEASONAL
Cocktails & Lovely Wines
MONDAY to
FRIDAY 5PM – 7PM

STAINBECK CORNER – HARROGATE RD
CHAPEL ALLERTON
T +44 (0) 113 307 0111
WWW.HUMMINGBIRDKITCHEN.CO.UK

The HUMMINGBIRD
KITCHEN AND BAR

OGI DAMJANOVIC
BAR MANAGER

T +44 (0) 113 307 0111
M +44 (0) 773 778 3195
OGI.DAMJANOVIC@HUMMINGBIRDKITCHEN.CO.UK
STAINBECK CORNER – HARROGATE RD
CHAPEL ALLERTON
WWW.HUMMINGBIRDKITCHEN.CO.UK

The HUMMINGBIRD
KITCHEN AND BAR

Small PLATES

EAST COAST SQUID £4.25	**SOMERSET BRIE FONDUE**
Lemon crumbs, sorrel mayonnaise and caper puree	Local asparagus, walnut scones and button
ALE BATTERED COD CHEEKS £4.25	**SLOW COOKED OX HEART**
'Yorkshire caviar', curry sauce	with celeriac and horseradish
HUMMINGBIRD CURE £4.25	**SUMMER SALAD**

MAIN Courses

HOMEMADE POTATO GNOCCHI £9.25	**SPICED BUTTERNUT SQUASH & ORZO**
Woodland mushrooms, baby spinach, Madeira cream and fresh herbs (v)	Black Sticks Blue cheese fritters, toasted se and watercress
CRAYFISH & EAST COAST MACKEREL FISHCAKE £9.25	**SLOW COOKED MIDDLE WHITE BELLY PORK**
Deep fried free-range egg, curry mayonnaise, watercress salad	Homemade black pudding, mustard mash, and apple puree
FILLET OF SUSTAINABLY SOURCED SEA BASS £13.25	**SWILLINGTON FARM FREE RANGE CHICKEN**
Jersey Royals, shrimp butter and local asparagus	Confit leg with spinach, red pepper puree a

The GRILL

All served with a grilled tomato, mushroom, small stack of hand cut chips and red w
Today cuts are 55 day aged, supplied by our friends at the Ginger Pig, Pickering. * Ideal to s

	200g	300g	500g*
RUMP STEAK	£12.25		
ON THE BONE SIRLOIN		£17.25	£25.50
FILLET STEAK	£18.25		

Alternative Sauces - Different sauces with your steak? Please choose from the follow
Bearnaise – Peppercorn – Bone Marrow Gravy all £2.50

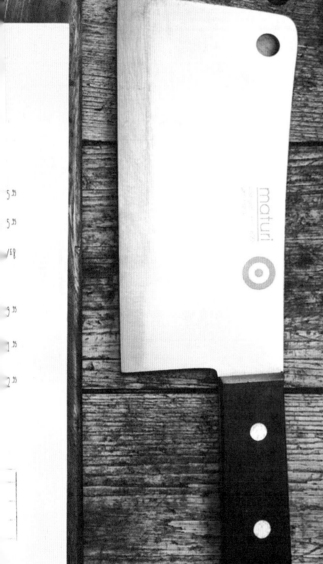

Bird Watching

Strollophone

The National

design studio
Love and War Associates

creative direction
Eng San Kho, Peter Tashjian

art direction
Katie Tully

design
Minh Anh Vo, Victor Schuft, Steve Fine

photography
Michael Guenther

copywriting
Peter Tashjian

Love and War's branding for The National restaurant brings chef Geoffrey Zakarian's vision of a "New York Grand Café" to life. The design is intended to be familiar and sophisticated, yet quirky and wry—a melting pot of characteristics befitting New York City's scene and culture. A key motif in the brand's design is a series of turn-of-the-century etchings that were reassembled into unique scenes and objects. These objects were then deliberately incorporated into the design sparingly to remain hidden for patrons to discover while dining, whether tucked away under a coaster or in between the pages of the menu.

The Pawn

design studio
C Plus C Workshop Ltd

The Pawn is a restaurant with a nod to all things British.
Located in Wanchai, it was originally a pre-war pawn shop
and has become a famous landmark in the district. To highlight
its uniqueness as a contemporary British restaurant and
strengthen the visual image of the brand, humorous pictures
and odd objects boost the restaurant's attractiveness and style.

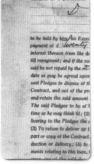

The Hayes

design studio
Paco. Branding & Design

creative direction
Judy Moosmueller

design
Judy Moosmueller

photography
Judy Moosmueller

The Hayes café is a small catering business. Care, honesty and dedication to quality are integral in its philosophy and are equally reflected through its design. The visual imagery of having a cherry on top logically associates itself to something cheerful and optimistic. The bright red cherry-shaped sticker functions as a cost-effective device that may be used on items that may not be easily printed directly on. A collage with illustrated food products was developed for other collateral to complement and complete the brand's visual identity.

BUY 8 COFFEES AND THE 9TH IS ON US.

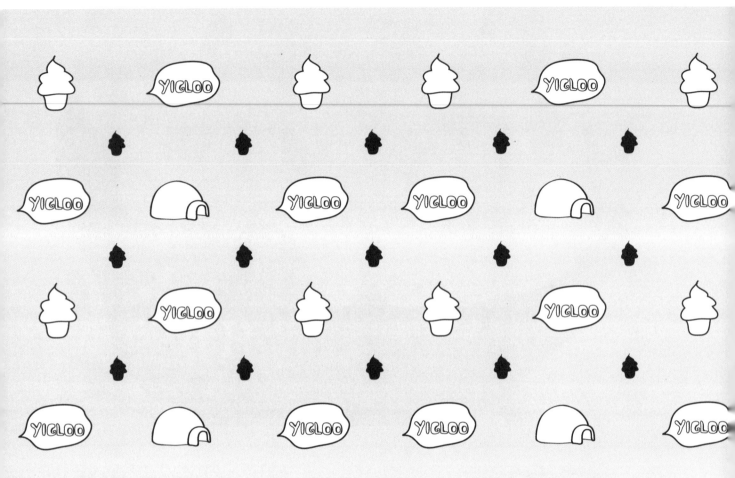

Yigloo

design studio
Foreign Policy Design Group

brand director
Arthur Chin

creative & art direction
Yah-Leng Yu

design
Cheryl Chong, Yah-Leng Yu

illustration
Cheryl Chong

space design
Weiling Lim, Minmin Choo from [+0]

Yigloo serves yogurt and revolves around the ideas of fun and happiness appealing to both children and adults. Whimsical and quirky characters were specially created and placed at unexpected corners in the store for customers to chance upon. These colourful characters, in contrast to an all-white interior, interact with the real environment. Refurbished and recycled furniture were whitewashed and re-used in the space, indicative of the joint's effort to be eco-friendly.

YIGLOO

MOMO

BONG

YOGGIE

TYLER

LET'S DO THE

PICK
A CUP

MIX
ANY FLAVOR

DRESS
ME UP

ENJOY
YUM!

fat-free true frozen yogurt
mix and match six flavors with

FREE
SAMPLING
COME ON IN

The Sweet Escape

A pleasant ambience forms the foundations of unforgettable dining and food experiences. Whether they are classy restaurants, cosy cafés or quirky ice cream parlours, the following pages are examples of well-designed interiors that allow diners to escape into whole new worlds.

DRI DRI

design studio
Elips Design

photography
Carlo Carossio

The Front Room of St Martins Lane's hotel is a dynamic retail space that has been converted into an idyllic Italian beach-style café that serves DRI DRI gelato. It is complete with traditional decking, coloured cabins, sun umbrellas, beach chairs and tables.

Kids Cafe Piccolo

interior design
PODIUM

graphic design
VONSUNG

photography
Interior - Budullee Lee (PODIUM)
Graphics - Yu-Kuang

The space of Kids Cafe Piccolo was designed and constructed by Design PODIUM in Seoul for children and their parents, consisting of a playground, playroom, party room, library and cafe. The identity of the café was created using Roman letters instead of Korean letters to make learning more enjoyable and interactive. In the play areas, lengths of timber floor planks were installed at perpendicular angles across one wall to create a series of rectangles and squares, reminiscent of a tree house. The playroom and library are painted in cool pastel colours to complement the flooring and bright furnishings while concentric circles are the highlight of the party room's ceiling. Majority of the café's walls are covered with educational graphics for children to play and learn simultaneously.

KIDS
CAFE 피콜로
PICCOLO

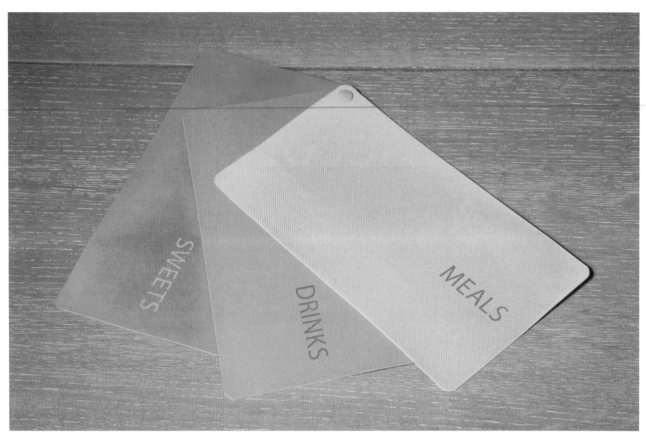

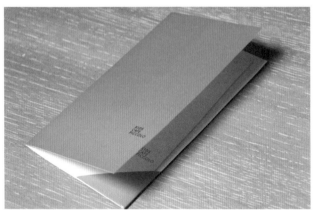

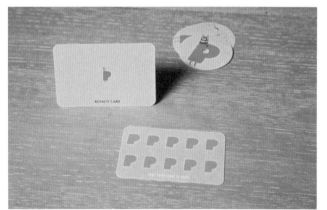

2F KIDS CAFE PICCOLO
02 2201-3252 kidscafepiccolo.com

Origin House & Kitchen

design studio
Studio Kudos

interior design
Andy Kim

photography
Eric Dinardi

Origin House and Kitchen is the first green café, grocery store and retail concept space to open in Bandung, Indonesia. Studio Kudos has crafted the brand identity and environmental graphics for the interiors and outdoor dining areas that would highlight the venue's emphasis on the green movement.

Cookie Scotland

design studio
de:strukt

design
Conzo Throb

illustration
Conzo Throb

The creative freedom allowed in this project has led
illustrator, Conzo Throb, to create imaginative worlds
of characters and detailed illustrations on walls, windows
and doors. Such refreshing quirkiness can also be found
in the restaurant's programme which showcases artists
and their works such as furniture pieces by eco designer,
Ryan Frank.

Agrioz

design studio
HOKO

in collaboration with
AMA studio

photography
HOKO

The Agrioz factory, located on the outskirts of Yilan City, is a major producer of premium candied fruit products. An adjoining warehouse, once part of the production factory, has been converted into a museum and café by Singapore-based design studio HOKO, in collaboration with AMA Architecture of Taiwan.

The museum was designed to communicate the individual elements and ingredients that make up the variety of candied fruit products produced exclusively by the family-owned company. Visitors to the museum are encouraged to smell and touch the different spices and fruits to gain a better appreciation of the use of natural ingredients in the process of making candied fruits. The café was designed to allow a generous amount of natural light and garden view, offering visitors a place to rest and enjoy refreshments.

Seventh Hill Pizza

design studio
Aesthetic Answers

creative director
Amy Herbert, Scott Herbert

photography
Amy Herbert, Scott Herbert

From the logo and interior design to packaging and signage, the award-winning Aesthetic Answers has managed to create a modern and inviting look for the bistro brand Seventh Hill Pizza. Deriving its name from the legend that all great cities are built on seven hills, the bistro prides itself in serving quality European pizzas. The bistro's focal point features a French made brick-and-stone oven, highlighting pizza-making's rustic appeal. In contrast, a modern bar surrounds the kitchen area, custom-designed out of reclaimed wood and metal with a concrete façade and oak countertops. Other interior design accents include bright yellow stools, custom menu boards, and window wells, with simple, crisp black and white checkered floor tiles. Traditional stained wooden pizza peels complement custom light sconces and a rotating exterior gobo light to create a dining ambience that speaks of the old and new.

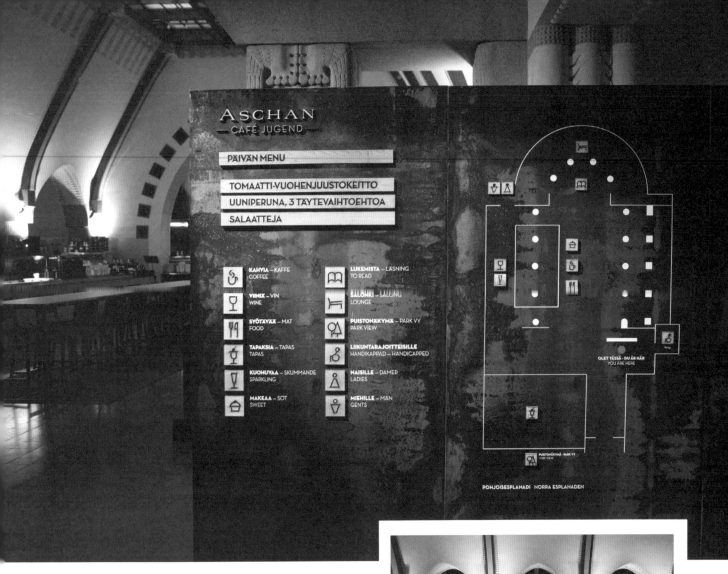

ASCHAN
CAFÉ JUGEND

PÄIVÄN MENU

TOMAATTI-VUOHENJUUSTOKEITTO

UUNIPERUNA, 3 TÄYTEVAIHTOEHTOA

SALAATTEJA

KAHVIA – KAFFE
COFFEE

VIINIX – VIN
WINE

SYÖTÄVXX – MAT
FOOD

TAPAKSIA – TAPAS
TAPAS

KUOHUVAA – SKUMMANDE
SPARKLING

MAKEAA – SÖT
SWEET

LUKEMISTA – LÄSNING
TO READ

SALONKI – SALONG
LOUNGE

PUISTONXKYMX – PARK VY
PARK VIEW

LIIKUNTARAJOITTEISILLE
HANDIKAPPAD – HANDICAPPED

NAISILLE – DAMER
LADIES

MIEHILLE – MÄN
GENTS

OLET TÄSSÄ - DU ÄR HÄR
YOU ARE HERE

PUISTONÄKYMÄ - PARK VY
PARK VIEW

POHJOISESPLANADI   NORRA ESPLANADEN

Aschan Café Jugend

design studio
Bond Creative Agency Oy

design
Aleksi Hautamäki, Tuukka Koivisto, Janne Norokytö

photography
Paavo Lehtonen

The creative agency Bond was assigned to create the interior design and branding for Aschan Café Jugend. Located in the heart of busy Helsinki, the agency decided to introduce a breath of heritage and history into the café's modern design. The 450 square metre space consists of a café, a wine bar and a shop. Special attention has been paid to the overall lighting concept, designed to highlight the spatial details within the café.

1916 THE BANKING HALL WAS EXPANDED AND THE MAGNIFICENT PEACOCK STAINED GLASS WORK DESIGNED BY VALTER JUNG ON THE END WALL HAD TO GO. IT WAS SOLD TO SVARTVIK MANOR IN KIRKKONUMMI. THE WORK, HOWEVER, RETURNED TO HELSINKI THROUGH AN EXCHANGE OF PROPERTY IN 1974. TODAY IT CAN BE FOUND IN THE BANKING HALL OF THE CITY TREASURY (POHJOISESPLANADI 15–17).

McVillage

design studio
UXUS

photography
Dim Balsem

UXUS was commissioned by McDonald's to create an inspiring, playful, educational and entertaining children's area within one of its outlets. The given area measured 20 square metres and adopted the theme "what I eat, what I do" where children can play and learn about food, replacing the existing ball pit concept common among European McDonald's outlets. It consists of a series of activities where children use their imagination to invent their own stories and games. This make-believe McVillage consists of three freestanding cottages: a farm, a market and a kitchen. This design emphasises the importance of educational and emotional journeys that occur when a meal is prepared.

Cielito Querido Café

design studio
Esrawe Studio

design
Héctor Esrawe, Ignacio Cadena

branding & graphics
Nora Cavazos Luna, Rocío Serna González

in collaboration with
Cadena y Asociados

photography
Jaime Navarro

interior (project leader)
Joaquín Cevallos

architecture
Arturo Gasca, Eduardo Álvarez

other collaborators
Sara Casillas, Ian Castillo, Jennifer Sacal, Roberto Escalante,
Didier López, Irvin Martínez, Cynthia Cárdenas

With Mexican and Latin American heritage, Cielito Querido Café
takes inspiration from the graphic expressions of the late 19th century,
vintage food labels, bold chromatic applications, and the work of
20th century Mexican artists, designers and architects. The use
of local popular expressions brings back the nostalgic spirit of old
grocery stores (Tiendas de ultramarinos/Tienditas de la esquina).

These elements were then fused with magnificent typography from
French and Spanish colonial times, resulting in a unique and playful
café steeped in nostalgia while still appearing urban, contemporary
and timeless. The interior, furniture and graphics were carefully
designed into little corners and details: the pinks, blues, blacks,
greys, typefaces, numbers, materials, flavours and patterned aphorisms.

D* Club & Cafe

design studio
Dopludo Collective

design
Lesha Galkin, Egor Kraft, Eibatova Karina

photography
Lesha Galkin, Egor Kraft

In St. Petersburg along the banks of the Gulf of Finland sits a small and cosy club and café. Its interior design consists of black murals on white walls and columns, leading to smooth transitions instead of hard corners across the entire inner façade. These black mural graphics illustrate scenes, images and mystical creatures from fairy tales and Nordic folk tales.

Merus

design studio
UXUS

photography
Dim Balsem

Merus underwent a transition from being a premium artisanal cult
wine to one of luxury status. UXUS was approached to design an
experience that would leave customers enveloped in the brand's
excellence. In order to create an interior that embodied Merus'
values of quality, sophistication and complexity, the design adopted a theme
that boasted a look of refined heritage with modern sophistication,
featuring classic monotone furnishings with contemporary finishes.
This eclectic mix of styles and periods combine to create an exciting
and unforgettable atmosphere. Objects such as wine barrels and
crates create compositions that subliminally inform customers about
the origins of wine, giving the space a sense of history.

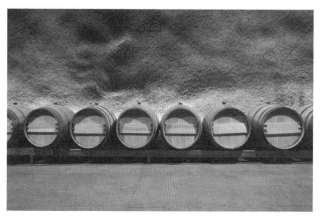

SOFT!

design studio
Bravo Company

art direction
Edwin Tan

design
Amanda Ho

Soft! serves smooth soft-serve ice cream that, using quality toppings, mix to form up to ten concoctions. The colour white was chosen as a base colour, alluding to the Japanese vanilla ice cream, and an illustrative style employed to represent the different flavours unique to Soft!. In line with this is the brand's marketing campaign that comes in a form of a Happiness Kit. It includes a Happiness Guidebook that recommends ice cream flavours as remedies for specific modern day stresses.

HAPPINESS GUIDEBOOK

SYMPTOMS & REMEDY

COMPLIMENTARY HAPPINESS

ONE FREE SOFT! SOFTSERVE ICECREAM

THE HAPPINESS KIT

REMEDY FOR THE BLUES

RASP
SPREE
RASPBERRY PUREE
SLICED ALMOND

$2.30

$2.30

CHOCO CHARM
CHOCOLATE FUDGE
CHOCOLATE CHIP
SLICED ALMOND
FRUITY PEBBLES

B1

$2.90

STRAITS CHENDOL
GULA MALAKA
CHENDOL JELLY
RED BEAN PASTE
FRUITY PEBBLES

B2

$2.90

GODZILL MAX
CHOCOLATE FUDG
OREO CRUMBS
MILO POWDER
FRUITY PEBBLES

B3

$2.90

BLACK FOREST
RASPBERRY PUREE
CHOCOLATE CHIP
SLICED ALMOND
SPONGE CAKE

B5

$2.90

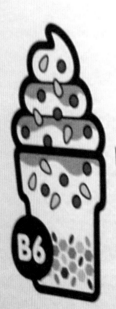

KIWI KIWI
KIWI PUREE
CRANBERRY CHUNKS
SUNFLOWER SEED
GREAT GAINS

B6

$3.30

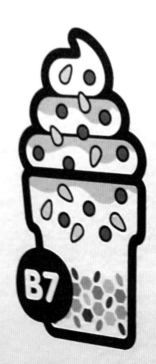

SUNNY ENSEMB
MANGO PUREE
CRANBERRY CHU
SUNFLOWER SEE
GREAT GAINS

B7

$3.30

Polka Gelato

design studio
VONSUNG

interior design
Joseph Sung

branding
Michiko Ito

photography
VONSUNG

Polka Gelato exemplifies creative director Joseph Sung's experimental playfulness with materials—lime concrete. Situated in a historical setting, Sung felt that juxtaposing old and new materials would give expected meaning for both, as seen in the use of the external architectural material of lime concrete within the interior space of the gelato store. Staying close to the idea of the Polka Gelato being an artisan store, Sung manages to avoid the unfriendliness of concrete. Instead, the smooth and clean interiors draw attention to the timeliness of the space, like being submerged in a tub of gelato. A circular passage allows customers to experience the space in multiple manners while furniture placed at strategic locations throughout the store renders the small space into an open and free one.

Viet Hoa Café

design studio
VONSUNG

interior design
Joseph Sung

branding
Michiko Ito

photography
Yu-Kuang

The main focus in designing Viet Hoa Café was to unify the space
in terms of colour and materials. The result was an earthy and neutral
palette accompanied by structured and distinct lines, reminiscent of
Vietnam's surrounding waterways and skies. A new identity system was
also developed by creating the "Hoa" (which means "blossoming flower"
in Vietnamese) logo that has been applied to the café's wayfinding,
collateral, packaging and uniforms.

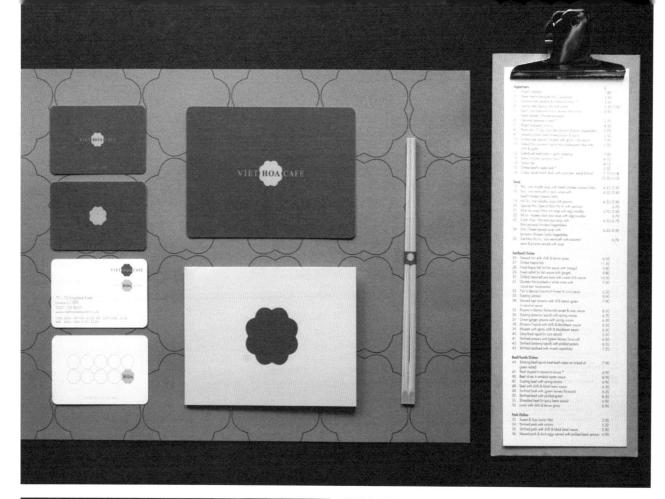

Peregrine Espresso

design studio
Aesthetic Answers

creative director
Amy Herbert, Scott Herbert

photography
Tyler Driscoll

Peregrine Espresso is known as one of the best independent coffee shops in Washington, D.C. Following the debut in its first location, the challenge was to design an environment that would be easily recognisable as part of the "Peregrine" brand, while retaining its distinctiveness. Reclaimed wood, concrete, drywall, exposed bricks and other reclaimed materials were central elements in creating a natural and relaxed environment, lending themselves to Peregrine's green initiatives. Also featured is a custom designed wooden seating area with quartz tabletops at the refurbished bay window and storefront, and a strategically located standing counter fashioned from quartz and wood wrapping around the thoughtfully planned shelves and drawers at the merchandise counter. In addition, a condiment and compost station allows for customers' easy access and convenient recycling of waste materials.

CurryUpNow

design studio
Design Womb

design
Nicole LaFave

CurryUpNow is known as one of the first food trucks in the
San Francisco Bay area. It specialises in authentic Indian street
food with fusion food twists. The mobile eatery currently has four
trucks and given its popularity among its bay area followers as well
as its rebranding it has finally opened a brick and mortar venue.

INDIAN STREET FOOD

Street Sweets

design studio
Landers Miller Design

design
Rick Landers, Colleen Miller

photography
Landers Miller Design

Street Sweets' visual identity is bold and fun, grabbing attention from the commuters along the busy streets of New York. Apart from this, it also presents itself with a level of sophistication through design and European-inspired influences in their offerings. It take cues from street maps and the hand-painted façades of traditional French pâtisseries that are known for their creative use of typography and texture. The mobile joint's visual elements consist of a round Street Sweets logo placed among horizontal and vertical grids of bold graphics and text set in Hoefler and Frere-Jones' Cyclone typeface. This identity system enables the truck to make a strong impact, and is flexible enough to be applied to other aspects of the business such as its website, packaging and promotional collateral without having to rely on excessive photography or illustration.

Yummo Yogurt + Smoothies

design studio
Tad Carpenter Creative

design
Tad Carpenter

Yummo Yogurt + Smoothies is a dessert restaurant that offers
any and every topping under the sun to go with its specialty yogurt
and smoothies. It allows the consumer to create, build and weigh
their own yogurt masterpiece and pay accordingly. This element
of personalisation has been applied to the design of the restaurant's
branding and identity, coupled with a friendly mascot and colour palette.

1221 WALNUT | KANSAS CITY, MISSOURI
P 816.221.4242 | W www.yummoyogurt.com

1221 WALNUT | KANSAS CITY, MISSOURI
P 816.221.4242 | W www.yummoyogurt.com

Take Away, Please.

· ·

The ingenuity of takeaway food carriers are often
overlooked because of their simplicity. However, projects
showcased in the following chapter will reveal how design
can transform humble paper bags and cups into walking
billboards for a brand's philosophy and its food.

Beachy Cream

design studio
Design Womb

design
Nicole LaFave

photography
Elizabeth Barr, Toky Photography

The founder and co-owner of Beachy Cream wanted to capture the
fun spirit that enjoying ice cream and ice cream sandwiches entails.
Her inspiration was drawn from the 1950s and 1960s culture along
Malibu, California. After a design overhaul, the results were alternating
colour business cards with playful typography and vintage elements.
The website design hints playfulness and is inspired by surf board
stickers, postcards and summer imagery. Signage for a portable ice
cream cart and functional postcards are also among a long list of fun
and upbeat marketing collateral for the brand.

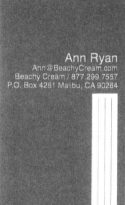

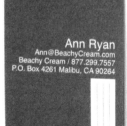

Backraum – Kipferl und so

design studio
Typejockeys

Backraum – Kipferl und so is a small bakery in Vienna that offers organic pastries, soups as well as design accessories such as bags, beanies, greeting cards and art works. Its logo has its typeface set in Aniuk and in bright oranges and pinks that stand out when applied to its food packaging, postcards, greeting cards, stickers, takeaway bags, stamps, flags and website.

Brown

design studio
Lip LTDA

creative direction
Lucho Correa

design
Oliver Siegenthaler

photography
Lucho Mariño

Opened in Bogotá, Colombia, Brown is a small confectioner's kitchen that offers a delicate selection of gourmet sweets. The design brief for the restaurant's re-branding specified a new corporate image with simple, low-budget solutions for patrons to easily identify with. In response to this brief, Lucho Corea created a series of cards and stamps that carry information about Brown, succinctly reinforcing the restaurant's philosophy of all things homemade.

Cake with Care

design studio
C Plus C Workshop Ltd

Cake with Care's philosophy is to make cakes that would play a part in enriching human relationships in daily life. Its name takes inspiration from the common expression "handle with care" usually printed on carton boxes. The same attention-grabbing sense of expression has been reinterpreted as modern illustrations that instead, exude fun and happiness.

Eat!

design studio
Bedow

creative direction
Perniclas Bedow

design
Perniclas Bedow

illustration
Axel Hugmark

Eat! Ekoaffären is Sweden's largest organic grocery store. Bedow design studio undertook the task of designing its visual identity, naming and overall store concept. Instead of simply placing a logo on a product or shopping bag, original illustrations and interpretations of the visual identity have been transferred to applications such as signs, bags, stickers, stationery, apparel, wall murals and packaging.

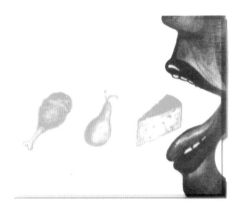

Oavsett om du föredrar en bit lagrad eller ett solmoget före den grillade så hittar du det hos .

Hjärtligt välkommen att handla för kr hos oss på Tegnérgatan 3.

Eat! Ekoaffären | www.ekoaffaren.se | Måndag–fredag.......07.45–20.00
Tegnérgatan 3 | info@ekoaffaren.se | Lördag...................10.00–19.00
111 40 Stockholm | Telefon 08-219 119 | Söndag...................11.00–18.00

Giltigt till: _____   Nr: _____

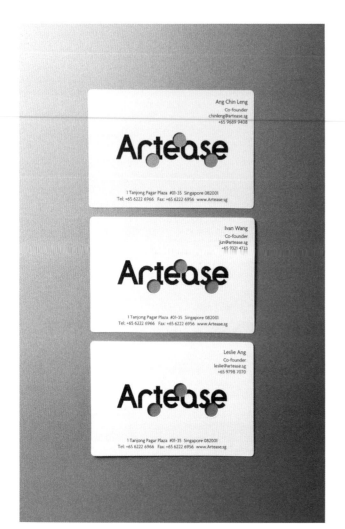

Artease

design studio
Splash Productions Pte Ltd

art direction
Stanley Yap

design
Lim Cailing. Jacqueline Ong

illustration
Eeshuan

motion graphics
Sang Don

Located in Singapore, Artease serves bubble tea, a popular
Asian milk tea drink that comes with sticky, chewy pearl-sized
starch balls. The three punched-out holes in its logo recall this
perfectly, paying tribute to the origins of the drink's name. A sense
of irreverence can be seen in a typically Singaporean mascot
and illustrations that can be easily identified with. The visual
identity of Artease has enabled this originally Taiwanese drink
to be a truly local rendition in a highly competitive market.

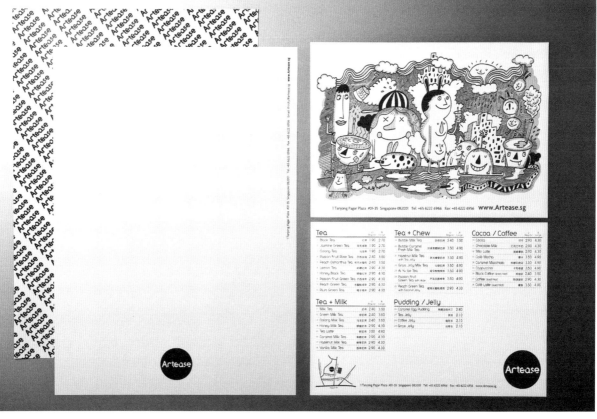

Brownice Vegan Ice Cream

design studio
Splash Production

art direction
Norman Lai

design
Lim Cailing. Terence Yap

web development
Lim Cailing. Terence Yap

copywriting
Terry Lee, Dominic Leong

It is a common misconception that all ice creams are not good for health. Brownice is a vegan ice cream made from real vegetarian ingredients. The ice cream's wholesomeness is expressed through its identity and collateral—with cursive typography, pastel blue and illustrations that recall classic ice cream stands of the past.

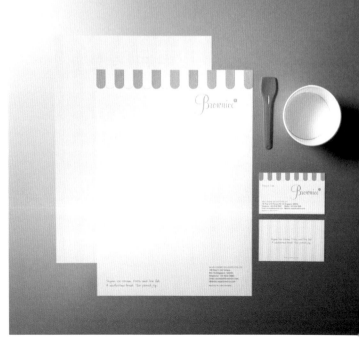

Hazelnut Chocolate

Banana Oats

Chocolate

Green Tea

Peanut Butter Caramel

Vanilla

Lavender Chocolate

Coffee Hazelnut

Pumpkin Coconut

Mulberry

Tropicana

Chendol

Durian

Lemongrass sorbet

Ginger tea sorbet

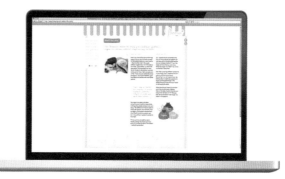

Brill.

design studio
Couple

Brill. is an urban takeaway food joint located
at small shop spaces where consumers expect
to be delighted and entertained while getting
their stomachs filled. Visually, the logo bears
a scalloped border that surrounds a combination
of Greek, checkered and cross-stitch motifs.

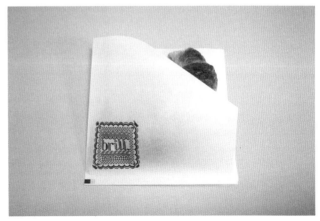

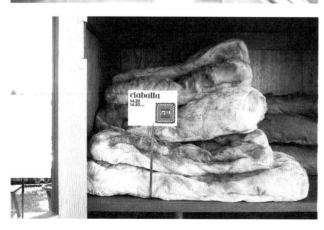

get a sushi

design studio
thisislove studio

design
Joana Areal, Inês Veiga

photography
thisislove studio, get a light™

thisislove design studio has designed a limited edition
takeout carrier that is accompanied by a Christmas gift wrap
and tablecloth with instructions to eat the sweet candy sushi.

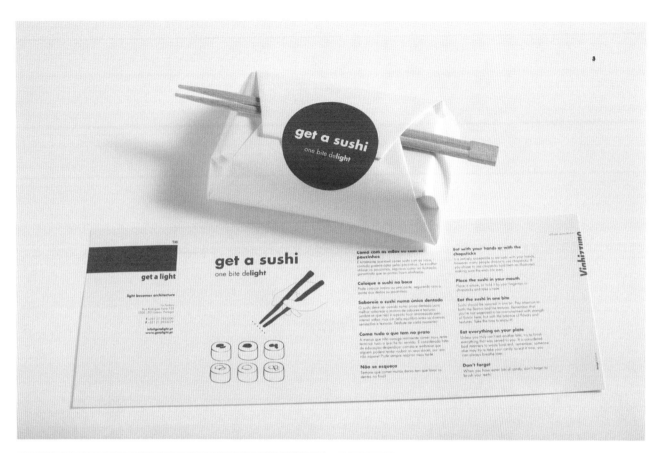

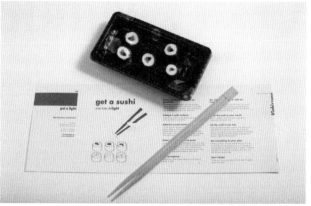

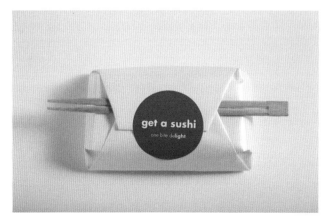

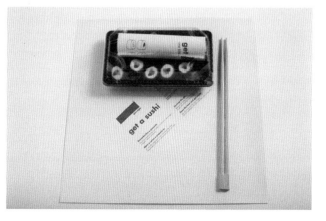

Minne's Diner

design studio
Sussner Design Company

creative direction
Derek Sussner

design
Brandon Van Liere, Jamie Paul

The Atsidakos family has been perfecting American and Greek comfort
foods such as pancakes, steak and eggs, ribs, homemade biscuits at
the restaurant, formerly named The Cottage Grill. Due to the success
of its new preservative-free apple pie, the restaurant was renamed
Minne's diner with the pie's logo and identity redesigned. In addition,
the main logo, menu, signage and website were re-designed as well
to focus on the family's recipe and flavours of naturally-made pies.

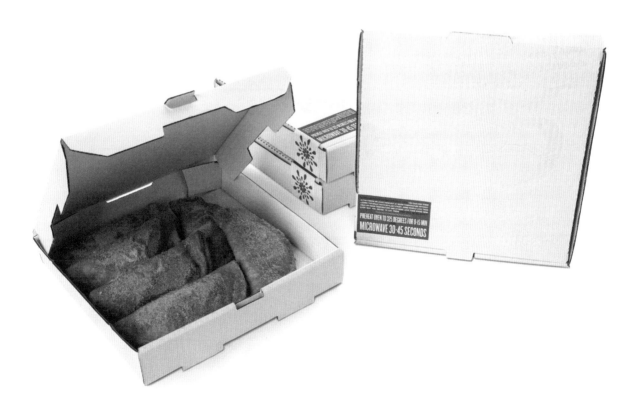

Jing An Bakery

design studio
C Plus C Workshop Ltd

Jing An Bakery is a large bakery chain in Shanghai
with 20 years of history and over 70 outlets. The prime
objective of its brand design is to project an image
of youthfulness and consistency in all outlets. Jing
An's logo design drew from the form of the typeface
used from Old and New Shanghai styles. In doing so,
it highlights the progressiveness of the bakery.

Make Shake

design studio
A Beautiful Design

Make Shake is a kiosk that allows you to create your
own milk shake concoctions from a variety of flavours
and mix-in toppings. Customised stickers were created
for the milk shake cups to promote this unique concept.

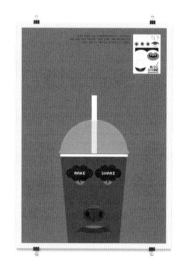
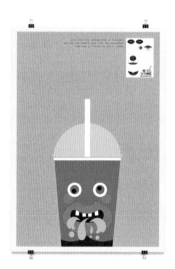

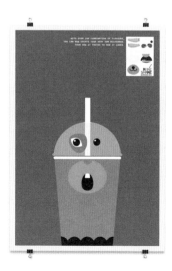

yogurt + mochi boutique

yogurt + mochi boutique

Maru Yogurt + Mochi Boutique

design studio
Studio Kudos

photography
Ervan Wifanie

other credits
Ervan Wifanie, Calvin Hao, Livia Ho

Located at the popular Plaza Indonesia, Maru yogurt and micha boutique specialises in serving Japanese frozen yogurt and mochi desserts. As Maru also means "circles" in the Japanese language, the design has employed circles as a dominant element from the logo to signage and packaging.

El Kombo

design studio
i'm a Kombo

in collaboration with
Surplus Wonder

photography
Oscar Meyer

El Kombo is a virtual Mexican Restaurant designed to bring the restaurant experienced home. The main focus for El Kombo's visual identity was to bring an extra dimension to the traditional take away experience through food packaging and food design. To make a strong first impression, a syringe was attached to the take away box and "injected" according to how spicy one would like the meal to be.

A string prompts one to pull open the box and be greeted by the delicious fragrances of the meal within. Arranged neatly is a typical Mexican meal and as a tin filled with warm food. A fork has been specially bent to double as tin opener while the garnish is on the right alongside the dessert and drinks at the bottom. Diners also have the opportunity to communicate with the chef and watch while he prepares the food in the kitchen via live streaming on the internet.

El Kombo

I'm a Kombo
Surplus Wonder

Moderado (Bo))

Medio)))

Intenso (Lasse)))))

Nr. 178 /

250

Pull

www.elkombo.com
Buenas
Noches
HOLA
Salud

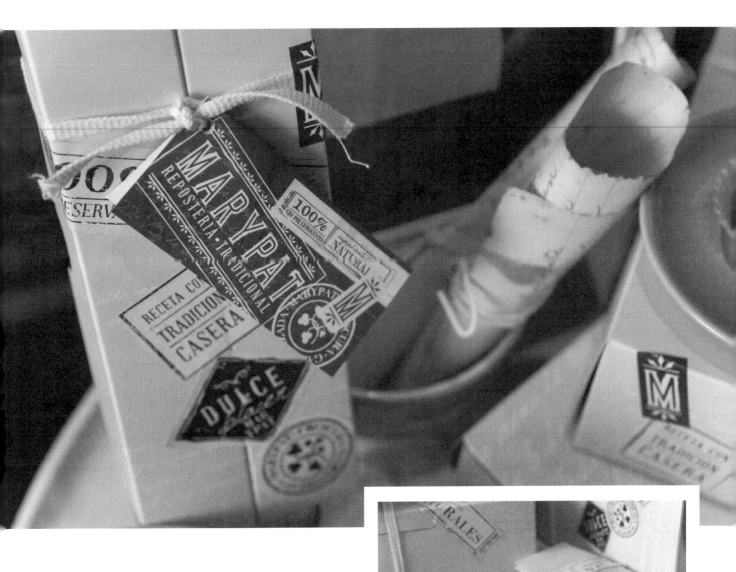

Marypat

design studio
Wallnut Studio

design
Cristina Londoño

photography
Alfonso Posada

Marypat is a sweet desserts maker whose visual identity has
been inspired by vintage French suitcases. Its identity consists
of specially designed stickers, stamps and cards. By mixing
these contents differently in each delivery box, customers are
always kept surprised by what they would find in their box of
sweet desserts. The packaging is available in various sizes to
contain small cookies, medium-sized desserts or large cakes.

Love Brownies

design studio
Supafrank

photography
James Champion

other credits
Jo Raynesford

Love Brownies is a luxury chocolate gift service that redesigned its
identity, packaging and website. It also worked with its designers to
identify the brand values that will be at the centre of all of its design
work. A standard box casing with a die-cut opening reveals hand-
written messages adorning a band within. This gives the recipient a
lovely surprise upon lifting the lid off the box. As the website is a core
vehicle for the brand, attractive copywriting and photography was
used to bring out the luxurious, heartfelt sincerity and hand-made
character of its brownies.

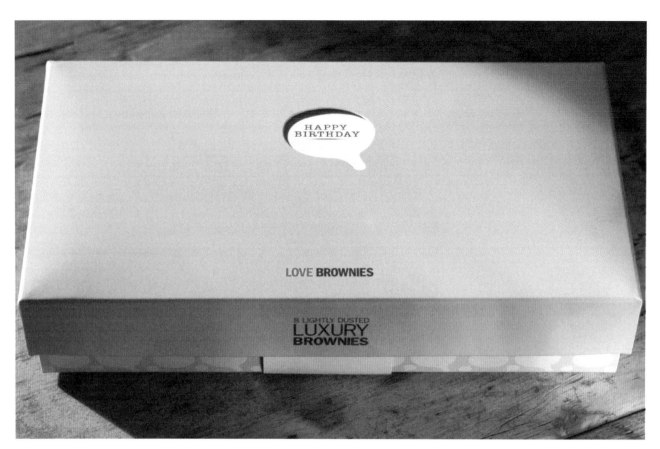

Lantana Café

design studio
Ortolan

photography
Etienne Gilfillan

illustration
Kat Macleod

Lantana is a café run by two Australians in London who aimed to create a strong mural and branding that would make it distinctively Australian—a sense of the wild Australian bush. The result was an interior with a seemingly unkempt environment adorned with unique wall illustrations of plants, bugs, beetles and birds. The mural covers the back wall and little bugs surprise customers and appear elsewhere on packaging. The logo bears the same hand-drawn and raw quality that conveys the café's similar culinary philosophy.

LANTANA CAFE
13 CHARLOTTE PLACE
LONDON W1T1SN
TEL: +44 0000 000 0000
WWW.LANTANACAFE.CO.UK

Pardon My French

design studio
Sussner Design Company

creative direction
Derek Sussner

design
Jamie Paul

photography
Robert Pearl

copywriting
Dave Schutz

Provided only with its location, a talented French chef and
his pastry creations, Sussner Design Company was asked
to redesign the identity of Pardon My French Bakery, Café,
and Wine Bar. The authentic French experience needed to
be demystified by developing a name and identity that was
inviting and light-hearted. By working with visuals associated
with French clichés, we were able to celebrate all things
French in a fun manner without being too serious. This
basic identity system resulted in modern aesthetics while
celebrating the heritage and traditions inherent in Pardon
My French's menu. These visuals were then consistently
applied to the design of its logo, table cards, signage,
gift cards and packaging, walls and window graphics.

La Madre Bakery

design studio
Swear Words

design
Scott Larritt, Sophie Good

photography
Cricket

stylist (photography)
Claire Larritt-Evans

La Madre Bakery proudly bakes traditional and organic breads with
a hands-on approach. This philosophy extends to its environmental
awareness and ethic, developing initiatives to reduce the eco-footprint
associated with baking. Design studio Swear Words has decided to
use this re-branding opportunity to inject more personality and unique
characteristics into La Madre's visual identity, which would set them
apart from competitors. Drawing inspiration from vintage flour tins of
the 1950s and 60s, the result is a visual language that is recognisable,
comforting and quirky, but still consisting of branding elements that
are scalable, flexible and adaptable for maximum shelf presence.

Saybons

design studio
Manic Design

Saybons French Food Factory is a kiosk that serves soups
crepes and breads with its visual identity and interiors designed
by Manic Design. With its food mainly prepared using traditional
French techniques, the base colour palette of red, blue and white
was chosen as a tribute to France's national colours. Located in
a busy area with high human traffic, the colour palette is adapted
to a pale turquoise to stand out without being too garish. A
recurrent pattern was created and applied across all kiosk
items—paper bags, crepe holders, and cups—for the colour
to become synonymous with the brand. The typeface has been
set in a stylish sans serif with distinctive wedge terminals for legibility.

saybons™

FRENCH FOOD FACTORY

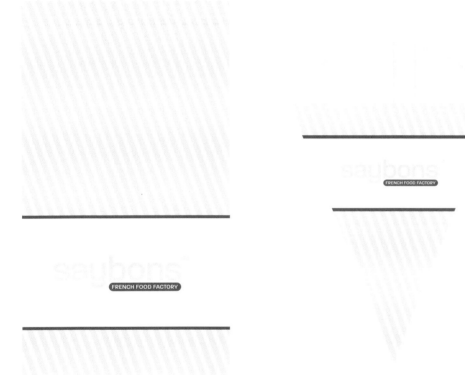

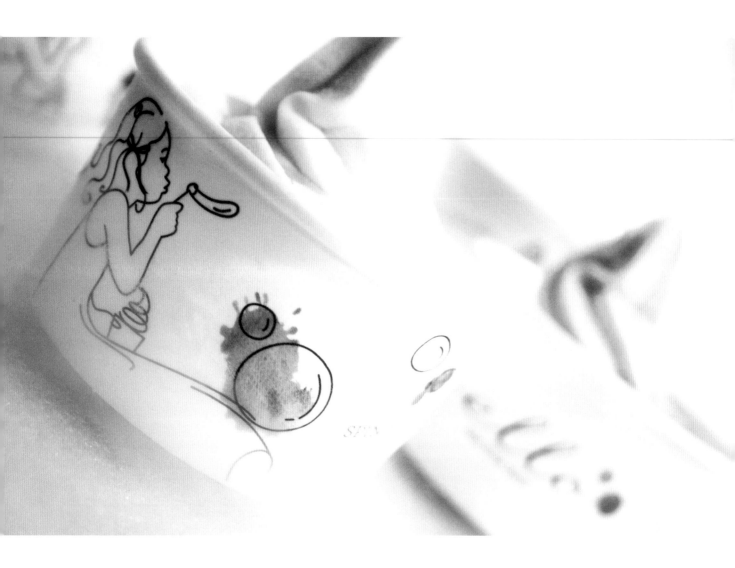

Oello

design studio
noote & netoo

Enjoying desserts such as frozen yoghurt has been associated
with bringing out the childlike innocence in people, and enjoying
the simple and fun things in life. Naming the yoghurt joint after
an ancient Incan goddess who was known for teaching the art of
spinning, the brand hopes to celebrate fun, tasty and fresh yoghurt
through its design as well.

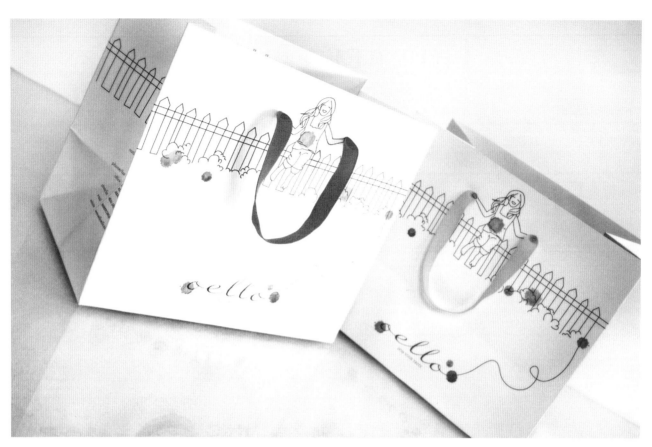

THEUREL & THOMAS
Maison du Macaron

THEUREL & THOMAS

THEUREL & THOMAS
Maison du Macaron

Theurel & Thomas

design studio
Anagrama

in collaboration with
Roberto Treviño, German Deheza

photography
Carlos Rodriguez

Theurel & Thomas is the first pâtisserie in Mexico to specialise in French macaroons, the most popular of the French pastries. The aim of this project was to create a brand that stood out, emphasising the unique value, elegance and detail in the making of this delicate dessert.

Using the colour white as the primary drive behind the design, attention is fully drawn to the colourful macaroons. By placing two irregular lines, one in cyan and one in magenta, the designers create an allusion to a modern version of the French flag—lending the vision and distinctiveness associated with flags to the brand's identity. A French typeface Didot (created by Firmin and Pierre Didot) was also used to give an added touch of sophistication to the overall design.

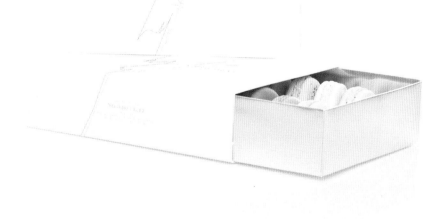

THEUREL & THOMAS

THEUREL & THOMAS

THEUREL & THOMAS

HEUREL & THOMAS

M Teafe

design studio
Studio Egregius

photography
Studio Egregius

M Teafe is a new destination for tea and coffee lovers.
Its fresh, new visual identity captures the bustling
yet personal atmosphere of Saigon's metropolitan
district. Inspired by the urban international icons of
the decades past, M Teafe's bold monochromatic
look is a fusion of the old and new. Studio Egregius
consistently maintains this look in a complete design
package, from paper cups to interior decoration.

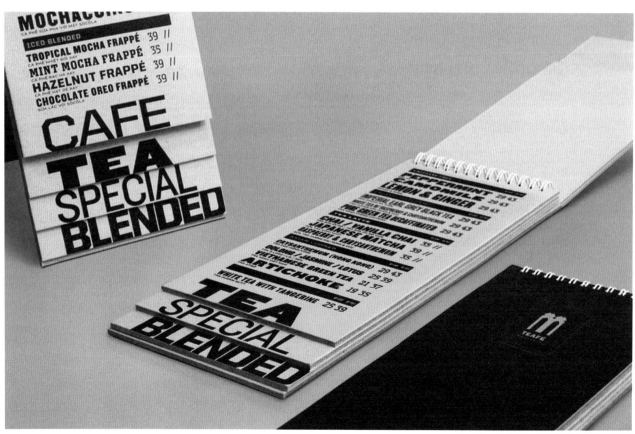

Slowly Does It

design studio
Berg

design
Daniel Freytag

Slowly Does It is a company that takes a passionate and no-
nonsense approach to food. To convey this, a robust typeface
and monochromatic palette was used on quotes from the owners
themselves, giving meaning and depth to the brand. These were
also applied to environmentally responsible packaging materials,
using craft paper stocks and excluding embellishments to deliver
its clean, simple and honest message: "It's all about the food".

Sullivan Street Bakery

design studio
Hyperakt

creative direction
Deroy Peraza, Greg Crossley

3D renderings
Jason Lynch

Sullivan Street Bakery makes some of the best bread in
New York City. Having been around for two decades, it is
considered a venerable institution among the city's culinary
circles with many top restaurants serving its bread daily. In an
effort to expand the bakery's products, a creative partnership
was set up with creative director Greg Crossley to develop
a packaging system that would extend the visual language
of the bakery across all current and future products.

box of 4 $12   box of 8 $24

we start with the finest ingredients: organic flour, sugar, eggs, butter, cheese, milk and cream to create a healthier, better tasting pastry.

früute

design studio
Ferroconcrete

photography
Vanessa Stump

Ferroconcrete was engaged as the creative force behind the launch of früute's mini tart revolution, creating a comprehensive identity system that was applied across multiple brand touch points: the store's interior design, environmental signage, its website and packaging. In line with Ferroconcrete's design philosophy, the identity system, brand language and tone were created to enhance früute's message and personality. The design direction for früute uses an exceptionally clean, modern and natural (thus the birch wood) aesthetic, bringing out the personality, colour and uniqueness of each tart. Its website showcases deconstructed tarts, featuring individual ingredients and details that make up the früute's artful masterpieces. Its takeaway box features a simple ribbon securing a lid with an image of a blue sky on the underside, a pleasantly surprising detail for anyone who opens früute's box of mini tart.

früute™ classic

three berries

lime meringue

passion fruit

baileys puff

yuzu

crème brulee

sea salt caramel

araguani

snowball

budino

pecan

tiramisu

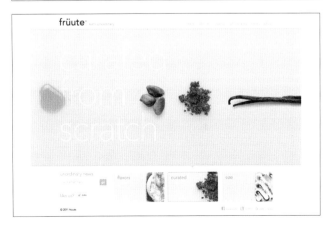

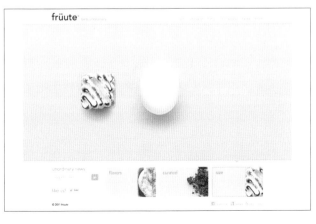

T&Cake

design studio
Build

creative direction
Michael C. Place

design
Lynne Devine

T&Cake is a modern café located in Yorkshire, the United Kingdom. In order to be differentiated from common tea-room style teahouses and to inject some fun into the brand, it required an identity that was versatile. Thus, the visual identity was designed to reflect this versatility that embodied the convenience of the café: accommodating dining-in, takeaway and small-scale retail shopping under one roof.

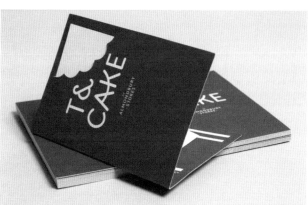

Fill Me Up

Some foods travel a long way to get to our supermarket shelves and onto our plates. From glass jars and plastic containers, to squeeze-out tubes and metal cans, this chapter features the best of food packaging designs.

Jimmy's Iced Coffee

design studio
Interabang

illustration
Chris Raymond

Jimmy's Iced Coffee's mission is to bring off-the-shelf iced coffee closer to people. The packaged coffee was launched in Selfridges & Co. departments stores, Harvey Nichols and then across most of the United Kingdom's supermarkets, shops and festivals. The packaging design has been infused with a sense of fun, boldness and retro styles using hand crafted typography. The design ensured that playfulness is a consistent quality throughout the brand's visual identity.

Alice & Jane's

design
Camila Drozd

Alice & Jane's is a bakery brand and shop inspired by the recipes of
the client's great great grandmother Alice, and Alice's mother, Jane.
The baked goods served are traditionally southern with an upscale
French flavour. Working with this specification, Camila Drozd developed
a French-styled logo, which bore a sense of hand-crafted originality,
much like the handmade goodness of the food. Affordable packaging
solutions were used, including simple containers, stickers, and labels.

The Butter Factory Myrtleford

design studio
Swear Words

design
Scott Larritt, Sophie Good, Paul Greskie

The Butter Factory's unsalted butter is hand-made using cream from
local high country cows and a unique blend of cultures in true European
tradition, while its lightly salted butter is made using Mt. Zero pink lake
salt. Designing the visual identity for this range of products thus, needed
to reflect the philosophical synergy of these two types of butter—
using only choice ingredients and paying exquisite attention to details.

Doves Farm

design studio
Studio h Ltd

creative direction
Rob Hall

illustration
Rosie Scott, Paul Desmond, Petra Borner

Being one of the pioneers of organic food in the United
Kingdom, Dove's Farm decided to undergo re-branding and
adopt a new packaging design to create a stronger presence
in the market. Responding to this, Studio h's work consists
of new product development and creating iconic packaging
that would make the brand instantly recognisable.

GLUTEN FREE

Chocolate
stars

cereal star shapes made with
organic chocolate, maize and rice

Space

| VEGETARIAN | VEGAN | ORGANIC | NO WHEAT | GLUTEN FREE | NO HYDROGENATED FAT |

STONEGROUND FLOUR
Wholemeal milled from an
ancient relative of modern
wheat, spelt will add delicious
complex flavours to all your
baking.

WHOLEGRAIN

Spelt flour

Spelt, triticum speltum, was widely grown in Roman
times. It is an ancestor of modern wheat and its
genetic heritage is a cross of wild grasses and early
cultivated cereals.

GB-ORG-03
EU Agriculture

GLUTEN & WHEAT FREE

Plain white
flour

gluten free white sauce, see recipes on reverse

| NO WHEAT | NO GLUTEN | NO ENZYMES | NO SOYA | NO NUTS |

GLUTEN & WHEAT FREE

White
bread flour

family pizza see recipes on reverse

| NO WHEAT | NO GLUTEN | NO ENZYMES | NO SOYA | NO NUTS |

STONEGROUND

Wholegrain
Spelt flour

olive bread, see recipes on the back

| ORGANIC | NO ENZYMES | NO SOYA | NO NUTS |

CULINARY

Pasta
flour

walnut ravioli, see recipes on reverse

| ORGANIC | NO ENZYMES | NO SOYA | NO NUTS |

BREAD FLOUR

Malthouse
bread flour

| ORGANIC | NO ENZYMES | NO SOYA | NO NUTS |

STONEGROUND

Buckwheat
flour

blinis, see recipes on reverse

| NO ENZYMES | NO SOYA | NO NUTS |

Nutella Esperienza Italia 150

design studio
ACR'S Srl

creative direction
Lino Bergesio

design
Mauro Ciani

3D rendering, postproduction & artworking
Angelo Iannuzzi

copywriting
Stefano Zimbaro

The design of the limited edition Nutella jar celebrates Italian excellence and is interpreted into four themes: the arts (music, poetry, cinema), design, landscape and architecture, and history. The result is a fresh set of whimsical dialogues between Federico Fellini and Moka, Rome and Venice, and Garibaldi and a Vespa. Here, words and design mingle and exchange places, forming rhythms of their own. This limited edition Nutella successfully embraces all things Italian with allusions to the North and South.

Sugar Skull

design
Catherine Bourdon

Sugar Skull is a Mexican house wine. Inspired by the Mexican holiday, El Día de los Muertos (Day of the Dead) and its traditional offerings, Sugar Skull's festive and unpretentious look was designed to stand out from traditional wine imagery. It features both a male and female skull to represent red and white wine bottles respectively. The skulls' design elements were deconstructed and rearranged to form a pattern that adorns the neck of the bottle, boxes and limited edition booklets that provides killer sangria concoctions.

A RED SANGRIA × TO DIE FOR ×

1 LEMON, SLICED
1 ORANGE, SLICED
3 TABLESPOONS BROWN SUGAR
1.5 OZ VODKA
1.5 OZ COINTREAU OR TRIPLE SEC
1.5 OZ GIN
1/4 CUP ORANGE SODA
1/4 CUP LEMON–LIME SODA
3/4 CUP PINEAPPLE JUICE
3/4 CUP ORANGE JUICE
1 CUP ICE CUBES
1 (750 MILLILITER) BOTTLE SUGAR SKULL VINO ROJO

VINO ROJO
12.5% 2010
MEXICO

SUGAR SKULL

VIVA LA MUERTE

Bogotá Beer Company

design studio
Lip LTDA

creative direction
Lucho Correa, Oliver Siegenthaler

design
Viviana Florez

photography
Doping

When Bogotá Beer Company came to Lip to renew their image, the latter saw a unique opportunity to utilise the company's old Ford truck that had been delivering beers to customers for the past eight years since its establishment. The names of Bogotá neighbourhoods were redesigned with emphasise on a strong typography set in Knockout and Univers to make a strong visual impact and establish a trademark look for the beer makers so well-loved by local Colombians.

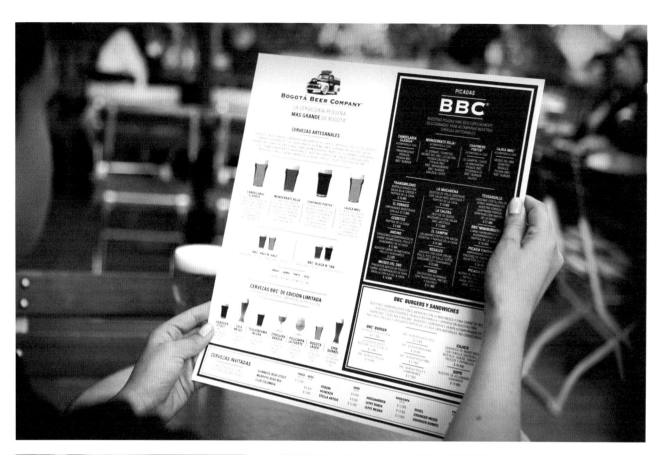

Carver's

design
Chris Schwartz

photography
Chris Schwartz

Carver's is a restaurant based off the work of George Washington Carver. The design, typography and materials used in this project were inspired by design from the era (early 20th century America) Carver was living in. Everything served on the menu is peanut-based and all designs are screen printed onto raw materials.

Green Eggs

design studio
Swear Words

design
Maureen Eu, Scott Larritt

Along with environmental sustainability and the humane treatment
of farm hens, Green Eggs prize freshness and quality above all
else. With the desire to share these values, it supplies only the
best to customers, and supports regional Victorian food producers.
Design studio Swear Words were tasked with the re-branding
and re-packaging of Green Eggs. The result is a fun brand that is
instantly understood for their values through their visual identity.

RNLI

design studio
Supafrank

photography
James Champion

RNLI aimed to broaden their appeal with their locally
sourced confectionery range and through a new packaging
design. The design brief was to engage with visitors across
the country and invoke in them reminiscence of the sea.
Images, scenarios and nostalgic elements of the British
seaside were visualised using simple and feel-good graphics.

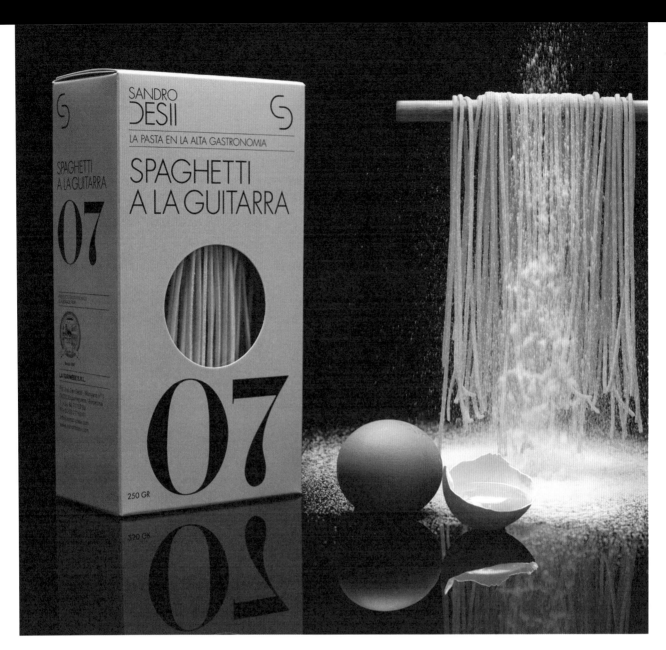

Sandro Desii

design studio
LoSiento

design
Borja Martínez

photography
Rodrigo Díaz Wichmann

The graphic identity and packaging design for the Italian pasta and ice cream manufacturer Sandro Desii has been designed by Borja Martínez from the design studio LoSiento. The logo is a symbol read as the letter "S" (representing Sandro) and consists of combining two "D" letters (representing Desii). When rotated at an angle, the logo will reveal two hidden "tongues", meant to signify the dual flavours of pasta and ice cream. The organisational system created using colour codes enable consumers and businesses to easily identify each product which comes with information about its qualities, colour, and historical numbering.

Villa de Patos

design studio
Savvy Studio

Founded in 1980 in the Mexican countryside, Villa de Patos is
a family business that provides organic and natural food products
such as fruit juices, artisan cheeses, and traditionally made Mexican
sweets. To reflect the tradition, purity and simplicity of the family's
line of products, a visual identity that embraced and projected the
Villa de Patos work ethic was developed. Freehand illustrations
of products, classic typography, and personal photo albums of the
owners make up the body of graphic elements used to convey the
brand's sincerity, acting as a contrast to quick and efficient consumption
as seen in supermarkets. These elements were applied to all its
communication materials, interior design, signage and packaging.

GÖTGATAN STORIES

TIDIGT VARJE MORGON BAKAR VI
BRÖD MED EKOLOGISKA RÅVAROR,
HÄLSOSAMT OCH UTAN ONÖDIGA
TILLSATSER. BAKVERKEN HOS OSS
ÄR VÅRA PERSONLIGT UTVALDA
FAVORITER.

HOS OSS HITTAR DU FRÄSCHA
SALLADER FRÄMST AV KRAVMÄRKTA
OCH EKOLOGISKA RÅVAROR. SPÄNN-
ANDE OCH SMAKRIKA TILLBEHÖR.
MEDELHAVSINSPIRERAT, EXOTISKT
... GISKT SVENSKT.

NJUT AV BIODYNAMISK JUICE
FRÅN SALTÅ KVARN ELLER BÖRJA
DAGEN MED EN NYTTIG SMOOTHIE
FRÅN INNOCENT, DÄR VARJE DRYCK
INNEHÅLLER MINST EN TREDJEDELS
KILO FÄRSKPRESSAD FRUKT.

VÅRT KAFFE ÄR FÄRSKMALET
BRYGGKAFFE I TVÅ VARIANTER.
KENYA AA ELLER RÄTTVISEMÄRKT.
ESPRESSOKAFFET ÄR EN BLAND-
NING AV ARABICA-BÖNOR FRÅN
INDIEN OCH GUATEMALA, 100
PROCENT ARABICA.

VÅRA BLOMTEER FRÅN NUMI HAR
... SENÄRIG TRADITION FRÅN
... ÅRE BIODYNAMISKA

Stories

design studio
BVD

creative direction
Carin Blidholm Svensson, Susanna Nygren Barrett

design
Johan Andersson

To create a strong and totally unique café experience: from concept and name, to graphic profile and packaging, this brand's design needed to be warm, welcoming, honest, genuine and targeted at young professionals. Black, white and stainless steel is combined with the use of warm wood. An old fashioned café ambience is created with simple details such as a message board with detachable letters, and traditional kitchenware and trays. The graphics are clean and simple, but at the same time surprising and playful. Despite traditional elements, BVD's design exudes personality, quality, style and a sense of being in the heart of city.

Fruita Blanch

design studio
Atipus SL

Fruita Blanch is a family business with a long tradition of growing their own fruits and turning them into jam, organic juices and preserved products. For its new product line featuring low-sugar, chemical-free, 100% organic and self-harvested preserved products, a versatile set of multi-sized labels were developed to fit every jar. These labels have been designed to reveal as much of the jar contents as well as to emphasise its artisanal nature.

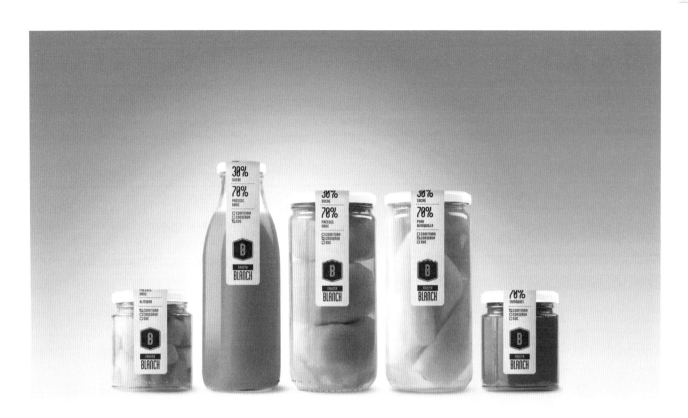

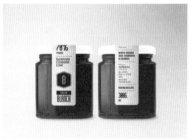

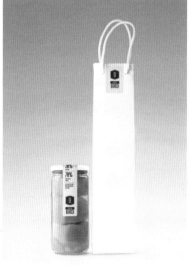

Healthy Choice

design studio
noote & netoo

Healthy Choice is a store dedicated to enrich people's knowledge
and awareness of healthy, natural and organic foods. The redesign
of its packaging has resulted in refreshing new colours that represent
different product categories, and highlight the products' nutritional
information. Taking into account that this market is particularly niche,
the packaging is simple, cost-efficient and easy to produce.

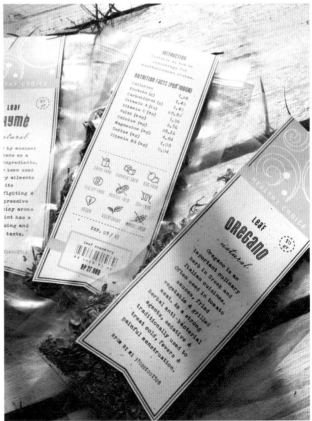

Index

Index

Index

Index

Index

Designlicious
Gastronomy by Design

Idea and Concept by

BASHEER
GRAPHIC BOOKS

Curated, Edited and Designed by

working title & co.

First reprint in 2013 by
Basheer Graphic Books

First published and distributed by
Basheer Graphic Books
Blk 231, Bain Street #03-61, Bras Basah Complex, Singapore 180231
Tel: +65 6336 0810 | Fax: +65 6334 1950 | www.basheergraphic.com

ISBN 978-981-071-577-9

Printed and bound by
Tiger Printing (Hong Kong) Co. Ltd

Acknowledgements
We would like to thank all the designers and companies involved in the
compilation of this book. This project would not have been accomplished without
their significant contribution. We would also like to express our gratitude to all
the producers for their invaluable opinions and assistance all this time.
This book's successful completion also owes a great deal to many professionals
in the creative industry who have provided precious insights and comments.
Lastly to many others whose names, though not credited, who have made a big
impact on our work, we thank you for your continuous support the whole time.

Future Publications
If you would like to contribute to our future publications, please email us at
hello@workingtitleandco.com